Macmillan Professional Masters

Cost and Management Accounting

D1147529

Macmillan Professional Masters

Law titles   Law Series Editor: Marise Cremona

Business titles

Cost and Management Accounting

Roger Hussey

Principal Lecturer, Bristol Business School

MACMILLAN

First published 1989 by
THE MACMILLAN PRESS LTD
Houndmills, Basingstoke, Hampshire RG21 2XS
and London
Companies and representatives
throughout the world

ISBN 0–333–44249–0

A catalogue record for this book is available
from the British Library.

Printed in China

10 9 8 7 6 5
00 99 98 97 96 95 94 93

To Jill

Contents

Preface

This book is written for managers and students who have no previous knowledge of accounting. Students studying financial accounting at the same time may find some of the concepts and approaches familiar.

I have set out to introduce the subject by using clear, simple examples and by avoiding technical jargon where possible. A sound foundation of the basic methods and procedures is laid down in the earlier chapters before examining the application of techniques.

At the end of the chapters there are questions, some of which may be answered by reference to the relevant text in the chapter or by referring to the outline answers included in Appendix C. Answers are not provided in this book to the questions drawn from the examination papers of the professional bodies. Terms printed in **bold** are defined in the Glossary in Appendix B.

ROGER HUSSEY

Acknowledgements

The author and publishers are grateful to the following for their kind permission to reproduce past examination questions:

Chartered Association of Certified Accountants (ACCA).
Chartered Institute of Management Accountants (CIMA).

The author and publishers are also grateful to the Chartered Institute of Management Accountants for their permission to use definitions from the *Official Terminology of Management Accounting* (1982), and to Chapman & Hall Ltd for tables from *Management of Company Finance*, 4th edn, by Samuels and Wilkes, 1986, p. 626.

Every effort has been made to trace all the copyright-holders, but if any have been inadvertently overlooked the publishers will be pleased to make the necessary arrangement at the first opportunity.

1 Introduction

1.1 The Need for Information

In a manufacturing company, it is easy to think of the types of financial information managers will require to be able to run the company successfully. First, they will want to know the *cost of producing the goods*. This information will be needed in some detail so that the costs of materials, wages and other items can be separately identified. Managers will want to know the cost of holding stocks of materials, the running costs of the factory, the cost of paying employees and the costs of other ancillary activities. Information will also be required on the *quantity and value of goods produced* and their *selling price*. All this information will enable managers to control the business activities, to plan operations and to make decisions.

The purpose of cost and management accounting is to provide information to managers which will help them to *control, plan* and *make decisions*. If cost and management accounting does not contribute to more effective management, it is of no value to the company and should not be undertaken. Experience has shown, however, that the discipline has much to contribute to effective management.

It is because cost and management accounting has shown itself to be essential to the running of a company that it has become so widespread; from the early times of manufacturing and trading, people have wanted information on the costs of running their business. At first, costing information was elementary, but as manufacturing industries became more complex, so the need for comprehensive cost systems and procedures grew. From being a record of what had happened, techniques developed which allowed managers to examine the financial consequences of *alternative courses of action* and to predict the financial impact of *future changes*.

The information needs of managers in manufacturing industries can be found also amongst managers in other industries and non-profit organisations. In the health service, the cost of providing various forms of care and support must be controlled within tight financial constraints; local authorities are increasingly interested in showing that they are providing value for money; the managers of banks, airline companies, charities and other organisations need information. The various techniques and methods of cost and management accounting, as explained in this book, enable the accountant to provide this information and advise managerial colleagues.

1.2 **Definition of Terms**

The topics of cost accounting and management accounting can be divided and studied separately. Because of the integral nature of the two subjects, however, there is an advantage in taking a collective view. **Cost accounting** is a part of management accounting. It is concerned with the collection and ordering of data to show the *actual costs* of operations, departments or products. **Management accounting** is broader in nature than cost accounting, a part of the *function of management*.

With cost accounting in its simplest form data may be collected only on past events; the costs *actually incurred* by the organisation in carrying on its activities will be identified and recorded. The costing system may provide such information as the cost of making one unit of production, the cost of running a particular department and the cost of scrap material.

In more advanced costing systems, *planned costs* will be decided before any activity takes place. The subsequent costs incurred can be compared with the planned costs, the differences identified and the reasons for these differences examined. In cost accounting, such planned costs are known as **budgets** and **standard costs**.

Management accounting encompasses the methods and procedures of cost accounting, with the purpose of providing information to managers so that policies can be formulated, activities planned and controlled, decisions on alternative courses of action taken, assets safeguarded, and the activities of the enterprise reported to interested parties.

In theory, and in practice, the division between cost accounting and management accounting is blurred. In general, cost accounting concentrates on the simpler techniques and the systems and procedures for collecting and analysing data. Management accounting adopts a more advanced approach, with a greater involvement in the process of the management of all the activities of the company. Because cost and management accounting systems and procedures within a company must be designed to meet the needs of the managers of that particular company, there will be a variety of systems in use in different companies. But at the foundation of all systems will be the requirement for cost and management accounting to assist managers by providing *relevant* and *timely information*.

1.3 **Control, Planning and Decision-making**

The activities of managers can be divided into three main functions to which cost and management makes a contribution. The first is concerned with the *control of the organisation*, both on a day-to-day basis and in the longer term. The second function is concerned with *planning for the future* and setting policies to ensure the success of the enterprise. Thirdly, managers are concerned with looking at *alternative courses of action* open to them, and deciding upon the preferred course.

1.3.1 Control

Most organisations have a number of control systems to ensure that progress is made towards achieving set objectives. In many companies there is a Quality Control Department to safeguard the fitness of the product or service. In manufacturing companies there will be some form of Production Control to monitor and coordinate the production processes.

Cost and management accounting provides the fundamental financial control system that is essential for the efficient working of the company. For control to be maintained, detailed information is required on such matters as the various costs of products and processes, the monitoring of labour efficiency and the identification of the sources and purposes of all expenditures.

1.3.2 Planning

Some form of control can be maintained by comparing present results with what has happened in the past. Unfortunately, as the business environment is subject to rapid change, such a retrospective comparison may prove of little value. The company may be currently operating in an economic climate very different from that of even a few months before. More rigorous control can be achieved by comparing present results with planned results.

Without plans and policies an organisation will have no sense of direction or purpose. Cost and management accounting allows plans and policies to be formulated in financial terms and provides managers with information on the *targets* and *standards* which the organisation intends to achieve.

1.3.3 Decision-making

Much of management time is taken up with making decisions on the company's present and future activities. In establishing plans managers have to decide which of the various possible courses of action they should take. Cost and management accounting supplies information on the *financial implications* of the various courses of action, thus helping managers to select the most appropriate one. It is at this more complex level of decision making that the emphasis falls on the techniques and principles associated with management accounting, rather than the simpler methods of cost accounting.

1.4 Methods, Principles and Techniques

Cost and management accounting establishes systems and procedures for collecting, analysing, summarising and presenting information to management. The methods adopted are determined by the organisation's business; the principles and techniques applied are determined by the *purpose* for which the information is required.

1.4.1 Costing methods

Costing methods can be classified into two main groups which are determined by the nature of production. **Specific order costing** is used where production results in units, or products, which are normally different from each other. The work produced consists of separate contracts or batches which can be easily identified.

Operation costing is used where the units are normally identical, or are capable of being made so by conversion. Operation costing is used when the goods or services result from a sequence of continuous operations or processes to which costs are charged before being averaged over the units produced during the period. Figure 1.1 illustrates how both these methods operate in the business.

Specific order costing can be broken down into *three* particular methods. Although they have much in common, each has its own specific requirements, depending upon the nature of the industry:

1. **Job costing** is used when customers specify their requirements and the job, normally *small in size and of short duration*, is mainly carried out in the company's factory or workshop. Although it may move through various operations, every job remains *identifiable*.

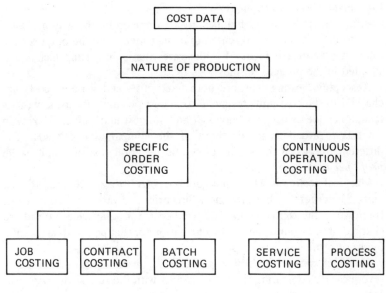

Fig 1.1 *Costing methods*

2. **Contract costing** is used when customers specify their requirements and the job, normally *large in size and of long duration*, is carried out on one site. This method is used widely in the construction industry.
3. **Batch costing** is used when a quantity of identical articles are processed as one batch. The batch is treated as one job and all the costs charged to it. The total costs for the batch are then divided by the number of good units in the batch to give an *average cost per unit*. Spoilt or scrap units are not included in the calculations.

Continuous operation costing can similarly be broken down into *two* particular methods:

1. **Service costing** is used when *specific functions or services* are costed – e.g., canteens or personnel departments. The method may be used to ascertain the cost of a service provided internally, or a service provided for external customers.
2. **Process costing** is where goods or services result from a *series of continuous processes or operations*. At each stage of the process, costs are charged before being averaged over the units produced during the period.

1.4.2 Principles and techniques

Costing principles and techniques are determined by the way in which the information is to be presented to management, and the purposes for which it is required. Figure 1.2 illustrates the main costing techniques adopted in the modern business.

Absorption costing is where both fixed costs and variable costs are charged to the cost units to give a total cost per unit. By using various techniques, described in Chapters 7 and 16, cost units are charged with what is regarded as a fair share of the company's overheads. The difference between the selling price and the total cost of a unit is the *profit per unit*.

Marginal costing is where the *variable costs only* are charged to cost units. The difference between the selling price and variable costs of a unit is known as the **contribution**. The fixed costs for a particular period are charged in full against the total contribution for that period to arrive at a figure of profit for the company.

Standard costing establishes predetermined standards for costs and revenues. By comparing the actual results with the standards, *variances* can be calculated and used by management to monitor progress and maintain control.

Budgetary control establishes plans in monetary terms which relate managers' responsibilities to policies. A comparison of budgeted with actual results leads either to managerial action to achieve the original policy, or to a revision of the policy.

Fig 1.2   *Costing principles and techniques*

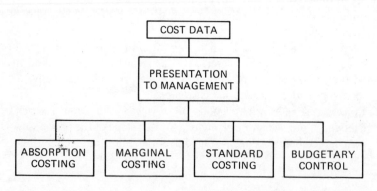

1.5 **The Role of Financial Accounting**

Financial accounting is concerned with classifying and recording *actual transactions in monetary terms*. The intention is to give a true and fair view of the financial progress of a company over a period of time in the form of *profit statement* and the financial position of the company at the end of that time in the form of a *balance sheet*. This true and fair view is usually intended for external parties – in particular, shareholders – although the information may also be used inside the company.

The transactions dealt with in a financial accounting system are varied in nature. Paying bills, collecting money from customers, paying wages and salaries and other crucial activities must be effectively achieved; even the simplest organisation must have at least a basic financial accounting system. Whether a cost and management accounting system is also present will depend on the information needs of managers and the financial sophistication of the organisation. It is usual for a simple costing system to be implemented initially and subsequently developed to include management accounting.

Financial accounting is governed by accounting concepts and conventions which have been established over a great many years. The financial accountant must ensure that information is prepared in accordance with *generally accepted accounting principles*. In large companies, this will entail compliance with legislation in the form of the Companies Act 1985 and meeting the requirements of **Statements of Standard Accounting Practice (SSAPs)**. These standards are issued by the Accounting Standards Committee and determine the way that certain matters must be treated in financial records and statements. The management accountant is concerned that information is of direct use to management and, to a large extent, has greater flexibility in the methods used for classifying and presenting information.

Although the financial accountant and management accountant may classify and use information in different ways and for different objectives, the same base of raw data is used. In companies where there is some form of cost accounting system in addition to the financial accounting system there is a strong relationship between the two. Both systems may be *integrated* into a single accounting system or there may be an *interlocking* system where cost accounts are maintained separately and reconciled periodically with the financial accounts (see Chapter 5).

In this book, financial accounting and the statutes and conventions surrounding it are not discussed. However, because of the close links in certain areas between financial accounting and cost accounting, some reference must be made to what are strictly financial accounting topics. For example, the appropriate valuation of stock held by a company is imperative in both systems and the methods to be used are covered in a Statement of Standard Accounting Practice and will be dealt with in Chapter 3.

The costing methods, principles and techniques will be examined fully in subsequent chapters. First, we need to explain what is meant by some of the terms used, and that is the subject of Chapter 2.

Exercises

1. What is the purpose of cost and management accounting?
2. Briefly describe the different costing methods used in the modern business.
3. How does cost and management accounting contribute to the other functions of management?
4. What are the main differences between cost accounting and management accounting?
5. Explain what is meant by the following:
   (a) Budgetary control.
   (b) Absorption costing.
   (c) Contract costing.
   (d) Specific order costing.
6. What are the main differences between financial accounting and cost and management accounting?
7. A friend, who is an engineer, owns a small factory and has relied on the annual accounts to show him the financial state of the company. You have suggested that he employs a Management Accountant, but your friend is uncertain how this will help the management team. Write a letter to your friend describing the management activities to which the appointed person would make a contribution.
8. A colleague claims that cost and management accounting is of value only in a manufacturing environment. Describe in which other organisations it would be useful, and give some examples to illustrate how it would be of value.
9. From the following list identify which activities are concerned mainly with *cost and management accounting* and which are concerned with *financial accounting*:

   (a) Drawing up the balance sheet of a company at the end of the year.
   (b) Calculating the cost of scrap on one of the product lines in the factory.
   (c) Ensuring that the accounts of a company comply with Statements of Standard Accounting Practice.
   (d) Estimating the energy costs to be incurred on a new project.
   (e) Keeping the records for the PTA at your local school.
   (f) Deciding which of the two proposed projects will be the most profitable.
   (g) Ensuring that PAYE records are correctly maintained in the company.
   (h) Reconciling payments made by the company with the bank statement.

(i) Analysing the reasons for the difference between the proposed material costs and the actual costs incurred.

10. Autovee Ltd is a small company manufacturing a range of motor vehicle components. The company sells approximately one-third of its production direct to motor vehicle manufacturers, the remaining two-thirds are sold as replacement parts through wholesale and retail outlets owned by the company. These outlets also sell vehicle components purchased from other manufacturers.

The only accounting data available in the company is that which is required to produce the company's published accounts, no accurate cost records are maintained and the auditors have suggested that the company would benefit from the introduction of a costing system.

Required:
Draft a report to the directors of Autovee Ltd explaining and illustrating how a costing system would assist the management of the company.

(ACCA, June 1980)

2 Cost Classification

2.1 **What is Cost?**

The cost of an item can be very hard to determine. A large part of this book is concerned with how we decide what is meant by 'cost'. The main difficulty is that our views of cost are influenced by our differing perspectives as buyer, seller or producer.

For example, if you buy a personal computer from the local store you might consider the cost to be what you paid for it. The storekeeper, however, may have a different opinion. Not only will the cost be what he paid the manufacturer for the computer, but he may wish to include a share of the costs of running his store: the rent, lighting and salaries, etc. He must be certain that his selling price is sufficiently high to cover these costs, to ensure that he makes a profit.

You may have bought a pack of 10 discs for your computer for £30. A friend wishes to buy one from you one Sunday for some urgent work he is doing. The original cost to you was £3 per disc, but you know that if you replace that single disc the following Monday, it will cost you £3.75. What will you decide is the cost, if you agree to sell to your friend?

Because the word 'cost' can be used with such varying interpretations, we normally try to make the meaning clearer. Cost used as a verb means *to calculate* the cost of a specified thing or activity; 'Cost' used as a noun means the *amount of actual or notional expenditure incurred on*, or *attributable to*, a specified thing or activity. But however the word is used it must be in context, and defined by specific terms or a classification.

2.2 **Cost Units and Centres**

Most organisations exist to provide an identifiable service or product. This output can be measured by devising some form of **cost unit**. This can be formally defined as a quantitative unit of product or service in relation to which costs are ascertained.

What the precise unit of quantity is depends on the type of industry, and cost units vary accordingly. In a brick works the cost unit may be 1,000 bricks, and costs are identified which refer to that unit. In a service industry the cost unit may be of a somewhat more abstract nature. A hospital, for example, may use 'patient-bed-occupied' as a cost unit and record all the costs relevant to that unit. A distribution company may regard a cost unit as a tonne-mile, so that the costs associated with moving one tonne of goods over one mile can be recorded.

As well as attributing costs to cost units, they can be attributed also to a **cost centre**. Any specific part of a company to which costs can be attributed may be designated a cost centre. It can be *geographical*, such as a department, or an *item of equipment*, such as a fork lift truck. Even a *person*, such as a consultant or a salesperson, can be a cost centre.

2.3 **Classification of Cost**

Costs can be classified in a variety of ways depending on the *purposes for which the information is intended*. These classifications help us to understand better what is meant by the word 'cost'.

2.3.1 **Direct and indirect costs**

A **direct cost** can be identified with a specific product or saleable service. Direct costs comprise direct materials used in the product, direct wages paid to the production workers for working on the product, direct expenses incurred on the product such as subcontract work, royalties or special tools.

An **indirect cost** is one which cannot be identified with any one particular product, but has to be shared over a number of products because it is common to or jointly incurred by them. Examples are rates, supervisors' salaries, consumable materials.

Some costs may be theoretically direct, in so far as it is possible to identify them with a product, but management find it more convenient to treat the costs as *indirect*. For example, some material costs may be insignificant and the value gained in identifying them with particular products may be outweighed by the inconvenience in attempting to do so.

Whether a cost is direct or indirect will depend on the analysis made at the time – in other words, what is being costed. For example, if a department is being costed, the supervisor's salary of that department is regarded as a direct cost. If one of the cost units passing through that department is being costed, the salary is regarded as an indirect cost. It is the focus of the analysis which determines the classification.

2.3.2 Fixed and variable costs

We will look more closely at fixed and variable costs in a subsequent chapter on marginal costing (Chapter 13).

Fixed costs are those costs which, in total, tend to remain the same *irrespective of changes in the level of activity* (which may be production levels). **Variable costs** are those costs which, in total, tend to change *in direct proportion to changes in the level of activity*. It can be seen from this explanation that direct costs will always be variable costs.

2.3.3 Classification by nature

It is essential for management to know the *nature* of the costs incurred. The basis classifications are materials, labour and expenses. These broad categories can be further subdivided; for example, materials may be broken down into raw materials, maintenance materials, etc. depending on the type of organisation and the information needs of managers.

2.3.4 Functional cost classification

Costs frequently relate to *specific functions*, such as the production function and the selling function. It is normally advantageous to classify them as follows:

1. **Production costs** are costs incurred from receipt of the raw materials to completion of the finished product.
2. **Selling costs** are costs incurred in creating demand for products and securing orders.
3. **Distribution costs** are costs incurred from receipt of the finished goods from the production department to delivery to the customer.
4. **Administration costs** are costs incurred in managing the organisation, but not specific to any of the other functions.

2.4 Elements of Cost

The *total cost of a product* is built up from a number of elements of cost. The correct classification of these elements is essential in understanding later topics, and students should *commit it to memory*. Figure 2.1 refers to a manufacturing company.

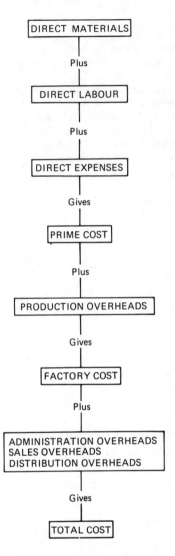

Fig 2.1 *Elements of cost*

Notes

1. **Direct materials** may be charged to the cost unit by a Materials Requisition or Stores Issue Note. The direct materials become part of the finished goods.
2. **Direct labour** converts the direct materials into the finished goods. The time spent on cost units may be calculated from time sheets, job cards or computerised records.

3. **Direct expenses** are not always present, but may be such items as subcontract work, or special tools or equipment bought for a particular job.
4. **Production overheads** are those indirect costs arising from the provision of the production resources. Examples are factory rent and rates, factory insurance, canteen costs.
5. **Administration overheads** are those indirect costs arising from the provision of the administrative function.
6. **Sales overheads** are those indirect costs arising from the selling of the cost unit – for example, advertising, salespersons' salaries.
7. **Distribution overheads** are those indirect costs arising from the activity of getting the cost unit to the customer, such as packing and transport costs.

2.5 Coding Systems

Codes are used so that items can be properly recorded, collated and analysed. To use descriptions only of the items would lead to ambiguities and difficulties in recording and processing the information. Although the appropriate classification of costs will have been determined by the company, the items need to be logically coded. For example, 5 centimetre brass plates may be coded as 05677, and no other class of item should be coded with that reference number.

The coding system will match the nature of the production process, the data processing and collection procedures and the purposes for which the information is required. A company will determine its own coding system, but the following characteristics are normally present:

1. The codes will be either *all numerical* or *all alphabetical*, with the former preferred.
2. The codes will be *brief*, have a *logical structure* and be of the *same length*, for example 5 digits.
3. There will be no ambiguities in the codes and the system must be such that *all items can be assigned a code*.
4. The code must be capable of *expansion* so that new items can be accommodated.
5. The control of the coding system will be *centralised* to avoid the proliferation and duplication of codes.

Exercises

1. What is meant by:
    (a) a cost unit;
    (b) a cost centre?

2. Differentiate between direct and indirect costs.

3. Describe the elements of cost.

4. What are the characteristics of a good coding system?

5. Explain the difference between a cost which is fixed and a cost which is variable.

6. Classify costs by function giving specific examples.

7. List the elements of cost making up the factory cost, with a brief explanation of each one.

8. A small company manufacturing garden furniture has drawn up a list of the costs it has incurred over the last 6 months. They are as follows:

	£
Wages	25,000
Electricity	1,200
Rent	2,000
Foreman's salary	6,250
Telephone	1,100
Timber	9,000
Insurance	500
Office salaries	5,000
Screws, bolts, glue	125
Rates	750
Oils and lubricants	175
Salesman's salary	4,200

Rearrange this list to show:

(a) The total cost for materials, labour and other costs.

(b) The totals of direct and indirect costs.

9. John Lesdon rents a workshop for £50 per week and pays heating costs of £15 per week. He has to pay insurance which costs £5 per week. John makes soft toys all of the same size and the costs for each toy are £2 for covering materials, 50p for stuffing materials and 20p for items such as eyes and mouths to sew on.

What is the total cost for each toy if John makes 70 toys in a week? What is the total cost if John makes 100 toys in a week? Why do these figures differ?

10. Classification and coding of costs:

(a) Distinguish between classification and coding of costs.

(b) What are the major requirements for a practical coding system?

(CIMA, November 1987)

11. (a) Define the terms 'cost centre' and 'cost unit'.

(b) Distinguish between direct and indirect costs, and discuss the factors which should influence whether a particular cost is treated as direct or indirect in relation to a cost unit.

(ACCA, June 1986)

3 Costing for Materials

3.1 **Introduction**

In many companies, particularly in the manufacturing industry, materials represent a substantial cost. Management establish procedures to ensure that:

1. The *correct quantities* of materials are ordered, at the right price and the right time.
2. The *correct materials* are delivered to the company.
3. Adequate arrangements exist to *store materials* until they are required.
4. Materials are issued from stores only with *proper authorisation*, and records are maintained of materials *issued* or *returned*.
5. A consistent and realistic system is operated to charge production with the *cost of materials used*, and to give a satisfactory valuation of materials in store.

A store often carries many hundreds of different types of materials, and to carry out all the above activities efficiently a considerable amount of paperwork or a sophisticated computerised system is required. Although companies devise systems and procedures most suitable for their own organisation, there are some standard terms for documents used. Figure 3.1 opposite gives an overview of the various stages, together with the names and purposes of the documents most commonly in use. The illustration assumes that a computerised system is not in operation, but in many cases computerised records are held. However, this does not detract from the general principles of the process and the need to maintain accurate records and controls.

3.2 **Purchasing Materials**

Purchasing is a highly specialised activity and includes responsibility for price, quality and time of delivery of materials. Ineffective purchasing

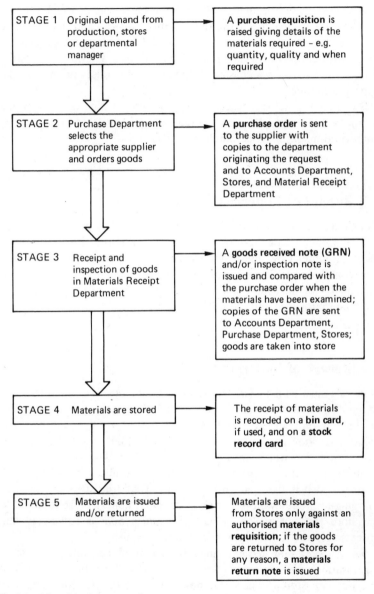

| STAGE 1 | Original demand from production, stores or departmental manager | A **purchase requisition** is raised giving details of the materials required – e.g. quantity, quality and when required |

| STAGE 2 | Purchase Department selects the appropriate supplier and orders goods | A **purchase order** is sent to the supplier with copies to the department originating the request and to Accounts Department, Stores, and Material Receipt Department |

| STAGE 3 | Receipt and inspection of goods in Materials Receipt Department | A **goods received note (GRN)** and/or inspection note is issued and compared with the purchase order when the materials have been examined; copies of the GRN are sent to Accounts Department, Purchase Department, Stores; goods are taken into store |

| STAGE 4 | Materials are stored | The receipt of materials is recorded on a **bin card**, if used, and on a **stock record card** |

| STAGE 5 | Materials are issued and/or returned | Materials are issued from Stores only against an authorised **materials requisition**; if the goods are returned to Stores for any reason, a **materials return note** is issued |

Fig 3.1 *Materials documentation*

has a direct effect on profitability; the purchase of the wrong quantity or quality of materials or late delivery can lead to *delays in production*.

The first stage in the process of material acquisition is that the Purchasing Department is informed that materials are required. This contact may come through the Production Department, which raises a *purchase requisition* specifying the quantity, quality, and delivery date for materials. In some companies a *schedule of material requirements*, specifying delivery dates and production needs over a period, is prepared and used by the Purchasing Department to raise orders at the appropriate time.

By using a purchase order, a *legal contract* is entered into by the company and its supplier; it is therefore imperative that only properly authorised managers issue purchase orders.

3.3 Receipt of Materials

Depending on the size of the company, materials may be received directly into store or there may be a special Materials Receipt Department. In either case, the materials should be examined to ensure that they comply in *quality* and *quantity* with the purchase order. A *GRN* is then made out and copies sent to the appropriate departments; the goods are taken into store and the GRN is signed.

3.4 Storage of Materials

Materials must be kept *safe* and *secure* and in a position where they can be *handled conveniently* and issued to production. Materials are issued to production only on presentation of a properly authorised *materials requisition*, showing the type and quantity of materials and the job or cost centre for which they are required. Stores pass the material requisition to the department responsible for maintaining the stock records and it is then passed to the Cost Department for pricing and charging to the relevant job or department. If materials are returned to the store for any reason, a *materials return note* is completed and processed in the same way as the material requisition.

Stock issues and *receipts* must be recorded accurately. In some organisations *bin cards* are attached to where the actual materials in question are stored. The card shows only the physical movement of materials, with receipts being entered from the GRNs and issues from the material requisitions. The card also shows the *balance of materials in stock*.

Because of the practical difficulty in ensuring that stores staff keep bin cards up to date, and the growth of integrated stock records and inventory procedures, which are often computer based, the use of bin cards is declining.

3.5 Stock-taking

Although adequate records may be maintained, for proper control it is essential that a *physical examination and count* of items in store is taken at intervals. With **periodic stock-taking**, the physical quantities of materials of all types is taken at a given date. This exercise, normally an annual event, requires a substantial amount of work and organisation; sufficient numbers of staff must be available who are fully instructed, and the stock-take may have to take place at a weekend so as not to disrupt production.

As a periodic stock-take is such a mammoth undertaking, many organisations use an alternative system. Staff are employed who carry out **continuous stock-taking** throughout the year. Some items of stock are checked every day so that all stock is checked at least once in a year. Fast moving and valuable items are checked a number of times throughout the year.

Continuous stock-taking offers many advantages, in addition to the absence of the need to halt production as with the annual stock-take. Trained staff without time constraints can be used, thus improving the quality of the work. The regular monitoring ensures that all staff adhere to systems and procedures, and any irregularities can be quickly spotted and rectified. This improved control will aid the efficiency of production and the profitability of the enterprise.

Some companies operate a **perpetual inventory system**, whereby the physical balance is calculated after *each receipt and issue of stock*. A record card is maintained for each item of stock showing the balance after every transaction. In this system there is continuous stock-taking to ensure that the actual quantities of stock agree with the records, and differences are corrected immediately. The advantage of perpetual inventory is that the stock levels at any time are known without having to conduct a physical stocktake. This information improves managerial control and decision making.

3.6 Stores Control

The cost of storing materials is very high, and it is important that *overstocking* is avoided, as this is a drain on the company's profits. However, it is equally essential that *understocking* does not take place, because a shortage of materials could mean a stoppage in production and a delay in meeting orders.

To avoid both these difficulties control is maintained by establishing *predetermined levels* for each item of stock. There will be a *maximum level* based on the storage space available, the rate of usage and wastage, the possibility of deterioration and the cost of storing above normal levels of stock. The *minimum level* can.be considered as a buffer stock. This is not normally used, but allows priority replenishment if stock falls to this level. The *re-order level* is the level at which a purchase requisition is made out to ensure that new supplies are received just before the minimum level is reached. The re-order quantity is the amount to be re-ordered in normal circumstances.

Even in the best organised and controlled stores losses may be revealed when stocktaking is carried out. Some of these losses will be unavoidable or the result of human error. Investigations should be conducted to find the cause of the loss, and any weaknesses in the system should be rectified. The losses must be valued and written off from the stores records with the authority of the manager responsible.

3.7 Pricing Issues and Stock

Establishing a price at which to issue materials from store is far more complex than it at first appears. The materials in store normally consist of several receipts at various dates, and these may have been made at a number of different purchase prices. It is often impractical, if not impossible, to identify each issue of materials with its corresponding delivery. It is therefore necessary to determine a method of pricing that is most appropriate for a particular company. All methods need a proper stock recording system. Five methods are commonly in use.

3.7.1 FIFO (First In, First Out)

This uses the price of the *first delivery of materials* to the company for all issues of stores until that particular consignment is exhausted. The next batch delivered is then used for the issue price. This therefore reflects good stocktaking practice, issuing the *oldest stock first*. As this method is based on *actual prices*, no fictitious profits or losses arise. Materials remaining in store at the end of a period are be valued at the latest delivery price and are therefore closest to up-to-date market values. This method is acceptable to the Inland Revenue, and is in accordance with the Statement of Standard Accounting Practice 9.

The FIFO system requires considerable record keeping, and does have some drawbacks. The issue price of materials may not reflect *current market values*; this means that product costs can lag behind current market values and different jobs may have different material costs, even when issues are made on the same day, thus making comparisons difficult. Fluctuating material prices also have an impact on product costs and profit: when material prices are rising, product costs are overstated and profits understated.

3.7.2 LIFO (Last In, First Out)

This uses the price of the *last delivery of materials* to the company for all issues of stores until that particular consignment is exhausted. The previous batch delivered is then used for the issue or 'last in' price until that has been exhausted or a new delivery received.

As this method is based on *actual cost*, no fictitious profits or losses arise. The value of issue is close to current market prices and the valuation of stock is usually very conservative. The basis of charging issues may mean that a number of batches in store are only partly charged to production where a subsequent batch has been received. As with FIFO, this system is administratively clumsy and comparison between the cost of different jobs is difficult. This method is *not* normally acceptable to the Inland Revenue, and is *not* recommended by the Statement of Standard Accounting Practice 9.

3.7.3 Replacement price method

This uses the *replacement price on the day of issue* to value materials issued from stores. This means that production is charged at *current prices*. As this method does not use actual cost prices, fictitious profits or losses may arise and cost comparison between jobs is difficult. It is difficult to keep up to date with replacement prices and this method is *not* acceptable to the Inland Revenue and *not* recommended by the Statement of Standard Accounting Practice 9.

3.7.4 Average price method

A simple average price may be calculated by adding all the different prices and dividing by the number of prices. This method is very crude and should be used only where the value of issues is low. A more sophisticated approach is to calculate the *weighted average price* by multiplying the prices by the quantities for each receipt and then dividing the total value by the quantities of stock held. The weighted average price is calculated only after receipt of a delivery of materials and not after each issue.

The weighted average method is somewhat simpler to operate than FIFO or LIFO, and being based on actual costs no fictitious profits or losses arise. This method is acceptable to the Inland Revenue and is recommended by the Statement of Standard Accounting Practice 9. It smooths out price fluctuations and cost comparisons between jobs are simpler. However, the issue price of materials is often fictitious in so far as it is not an *actual buying in price*, and issues may not necessarily be made at *current economic values*.

3.7.5 Standard price method

This uses a *predetermined (standard) price* for all issues and returns of materials. This method is simple to apply and as price fluctuations are eliminated the cost of different jobs can be compared. The setting of standards establishes a measure of control over purchasing operations. As it is not an *actual cost*, profits or losses may arise. The greatest difficulty with this method is in determining the *standard price* to be adopted.

Example 3.1

To demonstrate the impact of the different methods of pricing issues, the following information is used for the three methods requiring most calculation: FIFO, LIFO and Weighted Average.

Data:

    1 June received 100 kilos of materials at £2.00 per kilo
    2 June received 100 kilos of materials at £2.20 per kilo
    3 June issued 50 kilos
    4 June issued 60 kilos

The total stock on 2 June after the deliveries will be:

	£
100 kilos @ £2.00 =	200.00
100 kilos @ £2.20 =	220.00
Total stock 200 kilos	420.00

The effect of the three different methods will be as follows:

FIFO
The 50 kilos issued on 3 June will be priced at the first receipt price of £2.00 per kilo. Those issued on 4 June will be priced at £2.00 for 50 kilos, and as that exhausts the first delivery the remaining 10 kilos will be priced at £2.20 as follows:

	£
Stock held on 2 June	420.00
3 June 50 kilos @ £2.00	100.00
Value of remaining stock	320.00
4 June 50 kilos @ £2.00	
10 kilos @ £2.20	122.00
Value of remaining stock (90 kilos)	198.00

LIFO

The 50 kilos issued on 3 June will be priced at the latest receipt price of £2.20 per kilo. Those issued on 4 June will be priced at £2.20 for 50 kilos, and as that exhausts the latest delivery the remaining 10 kilos will be priced at £2.00 as follows:

	£
Stock held on 2 June	420.00
3 June 50 kilos @ £2.20	110.00
Value of remaining stock	310.00
4 June 50 kilos @ £2.20	
10 kilos @ £2.00	130.00
Value of remaining stock (90 kilos)	180.00

Weighted Average

With the weighted average method, the issue price is calculated on the *balance in hand prior to the issue of the materials*:

	£
Stock held on 2 June	420.00
3 June 50 kilos @ £2.10 per kilo	105.00
Value of remaining stock	315.00
4 June 60 kilos @ £2.10	126.00
Value of remaining stock	189.00

Note that the issue price on 3 June is calculated by taking the total value of stock at £420.00 and dividing by the total number of kilos to give the average price of £2.10 per kilo. If further materials were to be received at a different price the average price would change when the next issue were made.

Example 3.1 demonstrates in a simple manner how the pricing issue method affects the issue price and the value of the balance of stock held. Figure 3.2 illustrates the main method of pricing issues with more complex figures and using a format which is suitable for recording keeping and examination purposes. Dramatic price increases have been selected to emphasise the differences.

Data:

Date	Units delivered	Purchase price £	Units issues	Market price £
1/1	300	11.00		11.00
10/1	200	12.50		12.50
20/1			180	13.00
30/1			220	13.50
10/2	100	14.00		14.00
20/2			150	14.50

Standard Price £13

Method	Date	RECEIPTS			ISSUES			BALANCE	
		Quantity	Price £	Value £	Quantity	Price £	Value £	Quantity	Value £
FIFO	1/1	300	11.00	3,300				300	3,300
	10/1	200	12.50	2,500				500	5,800
	20/1				180	11.00	1,980	320	3,820
	30/1				120	11.00	1,320	100	1,250
					100	12.50	1,250		
	10/2	100	14.00	1,400				200	2,650
	20/2				100	12.50	1,250	50	1,400
					50	14.00	700		700
LIFO	1/1	300	11.00	3,300				300	3,300
	10/1	200	12.50	2,500				500	5,800
	20/1				180	12.50	2,250	320	3,550
	30/1				20	12.50	250	100	1,100
					200	11.00	2,200	200	2,500
	10/2	100	14.00	1,400					
	20/2				100	14.00	1,400	50	550
					50	11.00	550		

Method	Date	RECEIPTS			ISSUES			BALANCE	
		Quantity	Price £	Value £	Quantity	Price £	Value £	Quantity	Value £
REPLACEMENT PRICE	1/1	300	11.00	3,300				300	NOT
	10/1	200	12.50	2,500				500	USED
	20/1				180	13.00	2,340	320	
	30/1				220	13.50	2,970	100	
	10/2	100	14.00	1,400				200	
	20/2				150	14.50	2,175	50	
WEIGHTED AVERAGE	1/1	300	11.00	3,300				300	3,300
	10/1	200	12.50	2,500				500	5,800*
	20/1				180	11.60	2,088	320	3,712
	30/1				220	11.60	2,552	100	1,160
	10/2	100	14.00	1,400				200	2,560*
	20/2				150	12.80	1,920	50	640
STANDARD PRICE (£13)	1/1	300	13.00	3,900				300	3,900
	10/1	200	13.00	2,600				500	6,500
	20/1				180	13.00	2,340	320	4,160
	30/1				220	13.00	2,860	100	1,300
	10/2	100	13.00	1,300				200	2,600
	20/2				150	13.00	1,950	50	650

*To calculate the unit price, the average is calculated *prior* to the issue of materials based on the balance in hand

Fig 3.2 Main methods of pricing stores issues

Exercises

1. What is meant by perpetual inventory?
2. What are the advantages of continuous stocktaking?
3. What factors should be taken into account when deciding the predetermined maximum level of an item of stock?
4. From the following data, compute the value of 100 units of closing stock under both the FIFO and LIFO methods:

> 1 June Received 200 kilos at £15.00 per kilo
> 2 June Issued 150 kilos
> 6 June Received 200 kilos at £16.00 per kilo
> 9 June Issued 150 kilos

5. From the following stock records, value the stock held at the end of January using FIFO, LIFO, Replacement and Weighted average price methods.

Date	Purchase price £	Receipts	Issues	Balance
1 Jan	2.00			4,000
5 Jan			500	3,500
10 Jan	2.50	1,000		4,500
15 Jan			600	3,900
28 Jan			800	3,100

The replacement price on 31 January is £2.60.
6. Describe, and discuss the relative merits of, the various methods that may be used for pricing the issue of raw materials to production.

(ACCA, June 1986)

7. (a) Outline a suitable system for collecting the material cost of each job in a manufacturing company employing historic job costing.
(b) Zeppo Ltd manufactures a range of products from one basic material. In September the opening stock of the material was 650 kilos and, at the end of the month a physical count revealed a stock of 900 kilos, which was 250 kilos less than that shown by the inventory records. Except for the returns to the supplier shown below, all material recorded as being issued from store was consumed by production.

The material costs £2 per kilo. At the beginning of September the amount owing to creditors for supplies of this material was £3,800 and during the month Zeppo Ltd paid these creditors £7,200 and returned £600 of faulty material. At the end of the month the amount owing to the creditors concerned was £4,000.

The company operates an historic batch costing system fully integrated with the financial accounts.

Required:
(i) Calculate the value of material issued to production during September and record the month's transactions for the material in a stores account

showing both quantities and value. You should clearly indicate the account into which (or from which) the corresponding entry should be posted.

(ii) Briefly consider the possible reasons for the stock loss revealed by the physical count.

(ACCA, December 1980)

8. At the beginning of November the opening stock of a particular component was 440 units, total value £2,200.

During the month the following supplies were received:

8.11.1979	400 units, total value £1,800
15.11.1979	400 units, total value £2,200
22.11.1979	400 units, total value £2,400

There is a standard carriage charge included in the above amounts, of £100 per delivery, for transporting the components to the factory. The invoice for the goods received on 22 November had not been received by the end of the month.

Shown below are the issues from store during November:

2.11.1979	300 units	16.11.1979	500 units
9.11.1979	50 units	20.11.1979	20 units
13.11.1979	300 units	28.11.1979	30 units

The components issued on 9 November were used in the general plant maintenance programme and those issued on 20 November were incorporated into plant and equipment being constructed by the company's engineers to mechanise part of the manufacturing process. All other issues were made direct to production for inclusion in the output of the company's products, the issue on 28 November being to replace components damaged by incorrect handling.

On 21 November 40 units were returned to store from production and, at the end of the month, the closing stock was 440 units.

Required:

(a) Record the month's transactions in a stores account for this component indicating very clearly the account into which (or from which) the corresponding entry should be posted. You should assume the company operates an historic batch costing system, fully integrated with the financial accounts, and uses a first in, first out method of pricing material issues.

(b) Briefly contrast the effects of using first in, first out with the last in, first out method of pricing material issues from store.

(ACCA, December 1979)

4 Costing for Labour

4.1 Methods of Labour Remuneration

To understand labour costing it is essential to have some knowledge of the different *payment methods* operated. Specific company schemes present a variety of methods, but these can be broken down into two main groups: *time based*, where workers are paid at a basic rate per hour for the number of hours worked, and *performance based* (incentive schemes), where workers are paid on the basis of output or performance.

4.1.1 Time based

This method is easy to operate and avoids involving the company in the complicated negotiations which surround most incentive schemes. It is usual to set a number of normal working hours for a week and any hours worked in excess of this number are classed as *overtime*. These additional hours are paid at a higher rate – for example, time and a half: 1.5 times the normal hourly rate.

Example 4.1

A worker, who normally works a 40 hour week, is paid £2.00 per hour. Overtime is paid at time and a half. In one particular week he works 50 hours. What will his total gross pay be for the week?

	£
40 hours at £2.00 per hour =	80.00
10 hours at £3.00 per hour =	30.00
Total gross pay	110.00

As there is no pay incentive for high performance with time based schemes, close supervision and control is required. There is no incentive for workers to increase output, and there is a danger that they may unofficially operate 'slow' working in order to obtain overtime. Inefficient and efficient employees are paid the same rate as high performers, which may demotivate the latter.

To encourage good work performance a company may adopt a high *day rate scheme*. Work studies will establish an attainable output figure above the normal performance, and above normal rates will be paid to workers for achieving this. It is intended that such a scheme would attract higher grade workers by providing an incentive.

Problems may arise with high day rate schemes where the specified output figure is not reached, particularly if the fault is outside the workers' control – for example, material shortages and machine breakdowns. Management must ensure that adequate resources are available so that workers are not prevented from achieving their output figure.

There are circumstances where time-based schemes are appropriate. It is not always possible to measure the output of workers, so no targets of achievement can be set; the nature of the work may be such that care and precision are required and the company does not want workers to rush. It is argued also that time based schemes do not have any implications of exploitation and are more equitable, thus promoting higher morale and a harmonious industrial relations climate.

4.1.2 Incentive schemes
These schemes relate pay to performance. Because of the intricacies of some production processes, schemes can be quite complex in their nature. However, successful schemes attempt to relate pay *directly to a worker's performance*, be fair and achievable and easy to administer and understand. The implementation of such schemes will require negotiations and agreement with employees and any trade unions. This may take considerable time to achieve, with amendments being made to management's original proposals.

Incentive schemes present advantages by improving morale and increasing production through reward for extra effort. The potential for higher pay could attract more efficient workers and, in reducing the cost per unit, allow a company to be more competitive.

There are, however, difficulties in implementing incentive schemes, particularly in determining the required *performance levels*. Workers may regard specified rates as negotiable and any change in the production process may result in a fresh round of negotiations, and possibly disagreements and delays.

There are various schemes in operation, some closely tailored to a company's own needs. Typical examples of the more straightforward schemes are straight piecework and premium bonus.

4.1.2.1 Straight piecework
This is where the employee is either paid an agreed rate per unit for the number of units he/she produces or a piecework time allowed for each

unit. The worker is paid for the piecework hours of production, and piecework time is not the same as actual hours of work.

Example 4.2

The hourly rate for a worker is £2.50 per hour with an agreed rate of production of 250 units per hour. A worker produces 3,000 units in 8 hours.

If the worker is paid piecework on the basis of production, the piecework earnings will be the number of units produced multiplied by the rate per unit. As the rate per unit is £0.01 (£2.50 ÷ 250 units) the worker will receive £30.00 (3,000 units x £0.01).

If the calculation is done on piecework hours it will be:

$$\frac{\text{Units produced}}{\text{Hourly rate of production}} = \frac{3,000}{250} = 12 \text{ piecework hours}$$

12 piecework hours × £2.50 = £30.00

Variations of straight piecework may guarantee a *day rate*. This minimum rate will be paid if piecework earnings fall below it. The advantage is that workers are protected from loss of earnings through no fault of their own, for example material shortages and machine breakdowns.

Another variation is *differential piecework*, where the piecework rate changes at different levels of performance, usually measured as the number of units produced in 1 hour.

Although piecework schemes may be favoured because of the claimed advantages of high incentives, increased productivity and the possible reduction in the need for close supervision, the disadvantages may be onerous. Negotiations over piecework rates and allowances can be acrimonious and cause much delay and disruption. Schemes can be administratively difficult to monitor and operate and the complexities may lead to incorrect payments to workers. Often control systems have to be implemented to prevent abuse of the scheme.

4.1.2.2 Premium bonus
These schemes give a *time allowance* for a job and the time actually taken is compared with it. A bonus is paid to the workers on the time saved. The bonus is in addition to the normal daily rate, and therefore an incentive is offered to the workers for high achievement.

As the daily rate will be paid even if the time taken exceeds the time allowed, protection is given on the minimum amount of pay the employee receives.

4.2 **Recording and Costing**

The proper recording and payment of wages and control of labour costs are critical activities within a company. Procedures should be implemented and maintained to:

1. Ascertain the *actual number of hours* spent by workers on the factory premises. This permits control of attendance, payment of wages and control of labour costs charged to production activities. The term 'gate keeping' is used to refer to the records of hours spent on the factory premises, and in many companies a clock card is used, with each worker having an individual clock number.

2. Allow a *detailed analysis of labour costs* to show the production and other activities on which the cost was incurred. The time attributed to production activities should be reconcilable with the gate times.

4.3 **Time Sheets and Job Cards**

For recording time spent on production activities, a system must be devised to provide the maximum information required by the company for the costing system, but not incurring large administrative costs. There are two main methods of recording labour time. One is related to each individual employee through the use of **time sheets**. The other is related to each job through the use of **job cards** or **piecework tickets**.

4.3.1 Time sheets

These are prepared on a weekly or daily basis, employees completing the time sheets themselves and being countersigned by their supervisor. Daily time sheets encourage accurate recording and control, but lead to high volumes of paperwork and high administrative costs. Weekly time sheets are administratively more economical, but as employees tend to complete them at the end of the week, the accuracy of the information is influenced by their memories or imagination.

4.3.2 Job cards

A job card refers to a *single job* or *batch*. As employees complete their individual tasks on the job they record the time spent. A job card therefore shows a number of different employees' times, reflecting the passage of the job through a series of production processes.

4.3.3 Piecework tickets

These tickets refer to *each stage of manufacture*, so each job has a number of piecework tickets attached to it. This method increases the paperwork, but also permits the piecework tickets to be used promptly for wage calculation.

4.4 **Wages Office Procedure**

A *payroll* must be prepared giving details of every employee's pay. The *gross wage* is calculated from the clock cards for day rate and premium bonus workers and for the calculation of overtime payments. Piecework tickets and job cards are used to calculate payments to workers on incentive schemes. An *employee's record card* is maintained to show the remuneration details of each employee, including rates, allowances, tax codes and statutory deductions (see Figure 4.1).

Fig 4.1   *Typical labour recording system*

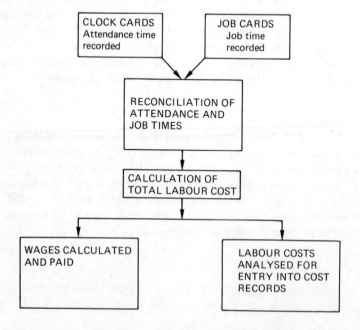

Exercises

1. What are the advantages and disadvantages of piecework schemes?
2. How are job cards used within a company?
3. A company operates a piecework scheme where the hourly rate is £3.00 per hour and the agreed rate of production is 600 units per hour. In an 8 hour day a worker produces 7,200 units. Calculate the piecework hours and the worker's pay.
4. What are the advantages and disadvantages of group incentive schemes?
5. The management of Fessil Ltd is reviewing alternative methods of remunerating its factory workers. At present all such employees are paid on a time rate basis and one suggestion being considered is the introduction of a piecework incentive scheme with a guaranteed weekly wage.

Required:
   (a) Describe TWO situations where piecework incentive schemes are unsuitable and the time rate method of remuneration more appropriate.
   (b) Discuss the advantages and disadvantages to management of introducing and operating a piecework incentive scheme.

(ACCA, December 1980)

5 Integrated and Interlocking Accounts

5.1 Cost Accounting Systems

All business organisations, unless they are very poorly run, must keep some form of *financial accounting system*. With some organisations (such as limited companies), there are very strict legal requirements; even with a person doing business on their own account the tax man will expect to see some form of financial records. In addition to the financial accounts many firms will keep *cost accounts*. Many firms will therefore need to keep two sets of books:

1. A *financial accounting system*, for recording such items as the purchase of raw materials, payment of expenses and the revenue collected.
2. A *costing system*, so that the total production costs can be accumulated and allocated to cost units.

There are a number of connections between these two systems. When a company purchases materials and records the transaction in the financial accounting system, those materials will form part of the cost of the product in the cost accounting system.

If you are going to maintain two systems you must ensure that they *agree*. It would not make sense to show different profits for a financial period from the two systems without being able to reconcile the differences. There are two ways of maintaining a cost accounting system to ensure that it agrees with the financial accounting system:

1. **Integrated accounts**, whereby the financial and cost accounts are *combined* through one unified accounting system. Only one ledger is kept, and this provides financial information for the preparation of financial statements as well as cost information for management. This system has the great advantage of not requiring any *reconciliation* between the cost profit and financial profit at the end of a period.
2. **Interlocking accounts**, whereby *separate ledgers* are maintained for financial and cost accounting. There are variations of the system, but normally the separate ledgers each have a *control account* which serves to interlock the two ledgers: there is a Cost Ledger Control

Account in the Financial Ledger and a Financial Ledger Control Account in the Cost Ledger.

5.2 **Integrated Accounts**

There are three main advantages of integrated accounts:
1. Only *one ledger* needs to be maintained, and no reconciliation between the financial and cost accounts is required.
2. The information generated can be used for *cost and management purposes* and for *financial reporting*.
3. The amount of *clerical work* is reduced, and *computer applications* are easier.

The two main disadvantages of integrated accounts are:
1. The rules relating to *stock valuation* for the financial accounts (lower of cost or net realisable value) may conflict with the methods used for *cost valuation*.
2. Cost and management accounting may require certain treatment of specific items which are not required for financial purposes. For example, overheads will normally be charged to production on a predetermined overhead rate (see Chapter 7).

The actual accounts used in any system will vary according to the size of the company and the nature of its system. In Figure 5.1 overleaf a very simplified illustration is given so that the main principles may be appreciated. The Overhead Control Account represents what would be a number of individual overhead accounts, and fixed assets have been ignored for the purposes of simplicity.

The general procedure in an integrated system is:
1. *Raw materials are purchased* and the Creditors Account will be credited and the Stores Control Account will be debited.
2. *Wages are paid* and the Bank Account is credited and the Wages Control Account is debited.
3. As production continues, so materials will be *issued from stores* with a credit to the Stores Control Account and a debit to Work in Progress Control Account. Indirect materials will be debited to the Production Overhead Control Account.
4. *Wages* will be credited to the Wages Control Account with direct wages being debited to the Work in Progress Control Account and indirect wages to the Overhead Control Account.
5. *Completed units* will be credited to the Work in Progress Control Account at the production cost and debited to Finished Goods Control Account.

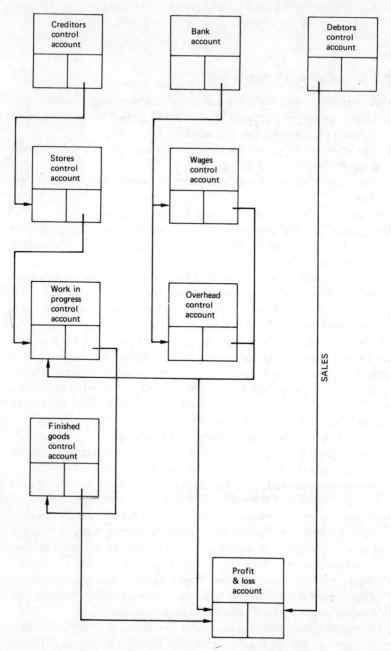

Fig 5.1 *Accounting flow in an integrated system*

6. The Finished Goods Control Account and the Overhead Control Account will be *transferred to the Profit and Loss Account.*
7. By recording sales with a debit to the Debtors Control Account and a credit to the Profit and Loss Account, the *profit* for the period can be calculated.

Figure 5.1 shows the system in a very simplified form, and the following worked example (Example 5.1) will demonstrate the operation of the system.

Example 5.1

A company is operating an integrated accounting system and at the beginning of a financial period the opening balances are:

	£	£
Raw materials	340	
Work in progress	90	
Finished goods	154	
Debtors	490	
Expense creditors		150
Trade creditors (materials)		340
Bank	100	
Fixed assets	600	

During the financial period the following transactions take place:

	£
Purchase of materials	220
Direct wages paid	125
Raw materials issued:	
To production	205
To maintenance	10
Material returns from production	5
Direct wages incurred	136
Administration costs incurred	84
Selling costs incurred	112
Production overhead incurred	207
Sales	840
Receipts from debtors	795
Payments to expense creditors	345
Payments to trade creditors	365
Cost of finished goods sold	515

Notes:

(a) Depreciation is charged at 2% of cost.
(b) Production overhead was absorbed at 150% of direct wages incurred.
(c) Work in progress was valued at the end of the period at £100.
(d) Administration and selling overheads incurred are charged in full.

Solution

Stores control account

£		£	
Balance	340	Work in progress	205
Creditors	220	Production overhead	10
Work in progress	5	Balance c/f	350
	565		565
Balance b/f	350		

Work in progress control account

£		£	
Balance	90	Stores returns	5
Wages	136	Finished goods	530
Stores	205	Balance c/f	100
Production overhead	204		
	635		635
Balance b/f	100		

Finished goods control account

£		£	
Balance	154	Cost of sales	515
Work in progress	530	Balance c/f	169
	684		684
Balance b/f	169		

Debtors account

£		£	
Balance	490	Bank	795
Sales	840	Balance c/f	535
	1,330		1,330
Balance b/f	535		

Expense creditors account

	£		£
Bank	345	Balance b/f	150
Balance	208	Administration overhead	84
		Production overhead	207
		Selling overhead	112
	553		553
		Balance b/f	208

Trade creditors account

	£		£
Bank	365	Balance b/f	340
Balance	195	Stores control	220
	560		560
		Balance b/f	195

Bank account

	£		£
Balance b/f	100	Wages	125
Debtors	795	Trade creditors	365
		Expense creditors	345
		Balance c/f	60
	895		895
Balance b/f	60		

Fixed assets account

	£		£
Balance	600	Profit and loss	12
		Balance c/f	588
	600		600
Balance b/f	588		

Wages control account

	£		£
Bank	125	Work in progress	136
Balance	11		
	136		136
		Balance b/f	11

Production overhead control account

	£		£
Stores	10	Work in progress	204
Expense creditors	207	Balance c/f	13
	217		217
Balance b/f	13		

Administration overhead control account

	£		£
Expense creditors	84	Profit and loss	84

Selling overhead control account

	£		£
Expense creditors	112	Profit and loss	112

Sales account

	£		£
Profit and loss	840	Debtors	840

Cost of sales account

	£		£
Finished goods	515	Profit and loss	515

Profit and loss account

	£		£
Cost of sales	515	Sales	840
Administration	84		
Selling overhead	112		
Depreciation	12		
Profit for period	117		
	840		840

5.3 Interlocking Accounts

In this system, the financial accounting ledger is maintained in the normal way with the debit and credit entries being made within the financial ledger, but no double entries span the two ledgers. The financial ledger will have a Memorandum Account known as the Cost Ledger Control Account which has posted to it all items which are to be *transferred to the cost accounting system.*

In the cost ledger there will be all the accounts for costing purposes – e.g., Stores Ledger Control, Wages Control. There will also be a Memorandum Account known as the *General Ledger Control Account.* This account ensures that the cost ledger is self balancing as it is a part of its double entry system. It should also agree, *but on opposite sides*, to the Cost Ledger Control Account in the financial ledger, thus providing the interlocking.

A typical entry in the financial ledger which interlocks with the cost ledger is the purchase of raw materials. In the financial ledger, the Creditors Control Account will be credited and the Purchases Account debited. In addition, the Cost Ledger Control Account will be debited. In the cost ledger, the Financial Ledger Control Account will be credited and the Stores Control Account debited. In Figure 5.2 a very simple example is given so that the main principles may be understood.

The following simple example shows the entries in the cost ledger for a financial period.

Example 5.2

A company operating an interlocking system has the following balances at the beginning of a financial period:

	£	£
Financial ledger control		3,300
Stores ledger control	596	
Work in progress control	1,760	
Finished goods control	944	

The following information is available for the period:

	£
Raw materials purchased	4,180
Direct wages	2,675
Indirect wages	420
Administration expenses	1,186
Selling expenses	725
Production expenses	625
Stores issues – production	2,862
– maintenance	173
Production overheads absorbed	1,140
Factory cost of finished goods	7,395
Cost of finished goods sold	9,162
Sales	10,700

Administration and selling overheads are charged in full for the period.

43

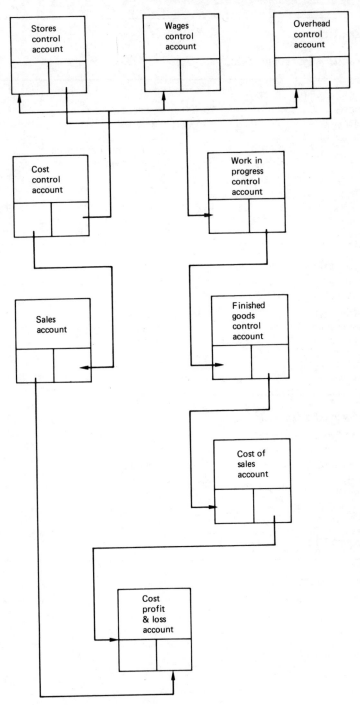

Fig 5.2 *Accounting flow in an interlocking system*

Solution

Financial ledger control account

	£		£
Sales	10,700	Balance b/f	3,300
Balance c/f	3,146	Purchases	4,180
		Wages	3,095
		Administration expenses	1,186
		Selling expenses	725
		Production expenses	625
		Profit	735
	13,846		13,846
		Balance b/f	3,146

Stores ledger control account

	£		£
Balance b/f	596	Work in progress	2,862
Financial ledger control	4,180	Production overhead	173
		Balance c/f	1,741
	4,776		4,776
Balance b/f	1,741		

Work in progress control account

	£		£
Balance b/f	1,760	Finished goods	7,395
Wages	2,675	Balance c/f	1,042
Stores	2,862		
Production overhead	1,140		
	8,437		8,437
Balance b/f	1,042		

Finished goods control account

	£		£
Balance b/f	944	Cost of sales	9,162
Work in progress	7,395	Balance c/f	363
Administration	1,186		
	9,525		9,525
Balance b/f	363		

Production overhead control account

	£		£
Wages	420	Work in progress	1,140
Expenses	625	Profit and loss	78
Stores	173		
	1,218		1,218

Administration overhead control account

	£		£
Financial ledger control	1,186	Finished goods	1,186

Selling overhead control account

	£		£
Financial ledger control	725	Cost of sales	725

Wages control account

	£		£
Financial ledger control	3,095	Work in progress	2,675
		Production overhead	420
	3,095		3,095

Cost of sales account

	£		£
Finished goods	9,162	Profit and loss	9,887
Selling overhead	725		
	9,887		9,887

Profit and loss account

	£		£
Cost of sales	9,887	Sales	10,700
Production overhead under-absorbed	78		
Profit	735		
	10,700		10,700

Closing trial balance

	£		£
Financial ledger control			3,146
Stores ledger	1,741		
Work in progress	1,042		
Finished goods	363		
	3,146		3,146

5.4 Reconciliation of Financial and Cost Ledgers

Some items appearing in the financial accounts will not appear in the cost accounts in an interlocking system. Examples are the purchase of a fixed asset, receipts of interest and dividends and profit on the sale of fixed assets. In addition certain transactions, such as depreciation and stock valuations, may be treated differently. Periodic reconciliations of the profits revealed by the two systems is necessary. The steps to follow are:

1. Begin with the *cost profit*.
2. Adjust for items appearing in the *financial accounts*, but not the cost accounts.
3. Adjust for any items appearing *only* in the *cost accounts*. This is unusual, but there may be notional charges for such items as rent.
4. Adjust for the different treatment of certain items such as *depreciation* and *stock*.

Example 5.3

A company's trading and profit and loss account is as follows:

Trading and Profit and Loss Account for the period ended . . .

	£	£
Sales		37,600
Profits on fixed assets		1,120
Discounts received		135
		38,855
Purchases	12,604	
Less closing stock	2,036	
	10,568	
Direct wages	5,200	
Factory expenses	6,124	
Administration expenses	2,675	
Selling expenses	4,038	
Depreciation	500	29,105
Net profit		9,750

In the cost accounts, the profit is shown as £9,200 based on the following information:

(a) Value of closing stock £2,200
(b) Selling expenses charged £3,600
(c) Depreciation £550
(d) Factory expenses charged £5,971

Reconciliation of profits

	£
Profit as per cost accounts	9,200
Add items not appearing	
Discounts received	135
Profits on fixed assets	1,120
	10,455
Adjust for difference in treatment	
Closing stock	(164)
Selling expenses	(438)
Depreciation	50
Factory expenses	(153)
Profit as per financial accounts	9,750

Exercises

1. Explain the main differences between interlocking and integrated accounts.
2. Explain, with examples, why differences arise between the profits in the financial and cost accounts in an interlocking system.
3. CD Ltd, a company engaged in the manufacture of specialist marine engines, operates an historic job cost accounting system which is not integrated with the financial accounts.

At the beginning of May 1980 the opening balances in the Cost Ledger were:

	£
Stores ledger control account	85,400
Work in progress Control account	167,350
Finished goods control account	49,250
Cost ledger control account	302,000

During the month the following transactions took place:

	£
Materials: Purchases	42,700
Issues	
– to production	63,400
– to general maintenance	1,450
– construction of manufacturing equipment	7,650
Factory wages: Total gross wages paid	124,000

£12,500 of the above gross wages were incurred on the construction of manufacturing equipment, £35,750 were indirect wages and the balance were direct.

Production overheads:
Actual amount incurred, excluding items shown above, was £152,350; £30,000 was absorbed by the manufacturing equipment under construction and under absorbed overheads written off at the end of the month amounted to £7,550.

Royalty payments:
One of the engines produced is manufactured under licence. £2,150 is the amount which will be paid to the inventor for the month's production of that particular engine.

Selling Overheads: £22,000

Sales: £410,000.

The company's gross profit margin is 25% on factory cost.

At the end of May stocks of work in progress had increased by £12,000. The manufacturing equipment under construction was completed within the month, and transferred out of the cost ledger at the end of the month

Required:
Prepare the relevant control accounts, costing profit and loss account, and any other accounts you consider necessary to record the above transactions in the cost ledger for May 1980.

(*ACCA, June 1980*)

4. Below are incomplete cost accounts for a period for which final accounts are to be prepared:

Stores ledger control

	£		£
Opening balance	6,000	(ii) Job ledger control	19,000
(i) General ledger control	27,000		

Production wage control

	£		
(iv) General ledger control	25,000	(v)	
		(vi)	

Production overhead control

(iii)		(x)	
(vi)			
(vii) General ledger control	19,000		

Job ledger control

	£		
Opening balance	20,000	(xi)	
(ii) Stores ledger control	19,000		
(v)			
(x)			

Selling and administration overheads

	£		
(viii) General ledger control	12,000	(xii)	

Cost of sales

(xi)			
(xii)			

Sales

	(xi) General ledger control	110,000

General ledger control

(ix) Sales	110,000	Opening balance	26,000
		(i) Stores ledger control	27,000
		(iv) Production wages control	25,000
		(vii) Production over-head control	26,000
		(viii) Selling and admin-istration overhead	12,000

The closing stock balances are:

    Stores ledger £12,000
    Job ledger £10,000

80% of the production wages incurred are charged directly to jobs. Production overheads are absorbed at a predetermined rate of 150% of direct wages, and selling and administration overheads at 10% of sales.

Required:
(a) Identify any distinguishing features of the cost accounting system.
(b) Complete the cost accounts for the period, by listing the missing amounts, determining the profit/(loss), and showing the balances to be carried forward to the following period.
(c) Provide a brief description of the accounting entries numbered (i) to (xii).

(ACCA, December 1986)

6 Overheads – Allocation and Apportionment

6.1 Introduction

At some point, a company may wish to know the *total cost* of a particular product or service. The records kept of direct costs, such as materials and labour, enable these costs to be identified with specific units. However, a company also incurs *indirect expenses*, such as rent and rates, light and heat, insurance and salaries of supervisors. Some method must be found to charge a fair share of these indirect expenses, known as **overheads**, to individual cost units to find the total cost of each unit.

The total cost of a unit may be required so that the company can set the selling price by adding a *fixed percentage*. This is very useful if the company is doing jobbing work or contract work where each job is different and therefore a common sales price cannot be used. Some people contend that the true profitability of different products cannot be ascertained unless the total cost is known. This is an issue that we will discuss at length in Chapter 16. It is certainly true that for controlling costs, fixing prices, submitting tenders, predicting future activities and making other decisions, management may find that knowledge of the total cost of a product is extremely valuable.

If a company consisted of only one production department and manufactured only one product, the method of sharing the overheads for a period of time over these products would be a straightforward task. The total overheads for the period could be divided by the number of cost units produced in that period to give an *average overhead cost per unit*. This figure can be added to the direct costs per unit to give a total cost.

In practice, organisations are far more complex than this. There may be a number of different departments (departments are called 'shops' in some industries) carrying out a range of activities. Some departments – the *service cost centres* – may not be directly engaged in manufacturing, but provide support such as maintenance facilities or the storage of raw materials and finished goods. Also the products themselves may vary, and spend differing lengths of time in the individual production departments, thus making unequal demands upon resources. In these instances, ways must be found to share the total overheads of the company fairly over the production departments and then over the cost units passing through them.

Absorption costing is a technique which allows us to charge overheads to cost units by means of rates separately calculated for each cost centre. It seeks to provide a solution to two problems:

1. How to share the total overheads of the company over the various *production departments*.
2. How to share the overheads for a particular production department over the *various products passing through it*.

In this chapter we look at the first problem – the sharing of overheads over the various production departments. The examples are drawn from a manufacturing environment, although absorption costing is used in other industries. In this chapter production overheads are examined, leaving consideration of non-production overheads, such as administration and selling overheads, to Chapter 7.

6.2 Overheads – Classification and Collection

Overheads are those costs which *cannot be identified directly* through the costing system with a job, product, batch or service, and therefore are the total of indirect materials, indirect labour and indirect expenses.

The definition a company uses for a cost unit affects what is classified as an 'overhead'. If a construction company is erecting a new building, it may regard it as the cost unit and such costs as supervision, site administration and power – normally regarded by a manufacturing concern as overheads – will be *direct costs* for that building. The construction may consist of a number of separate buildings, each regarded as a cost unit in its own right, thus requiring a different definition of overheads.

A further example is that of a special machine which may have been purchased. If it is used specifically on one particular job it is a direct cost, but if it is used on a number of jobs it should be considered as an overhead.

Another problem arises where it has been decided to work overtime on a particular job, with a premium paid to the workforce. The overtime premium is a direct cost if the customer's request necessitated the overtime working. If the overtime was to permit a general backlog of work to be cleared, however, the premium should be considered as an overhead cost.

Overhead costs are normally channelled through the accountancy system as part of established procedures. It is usual to classify the overheads by *nature* (e.g., indirect materials, depreciation, salaries) and, if possible, by *cost centre*.

When the overhead costs have been collected, they fall into two categories. There are those overhead costs which, in their entirety, can be clearly identified with one cost centre which are termed *cost centre direct costs*. Other overheads, which cannot be identified with only one cost centre, must be shared over the relevant cost centres. These two types of overhead costs require differing treatments, known as **allocation** and **apportionment**.

6.3 Cost Allocation

Overhead costs which can be allocated cause few problems and students should tackle these first in an examination question.

To allocate an overhead cost, the cost centre must have *caused* the overhead to have been incurred, and the *exact amount* must be known.

The ability to allocate overhead costs depends, to some extent, upon the sophistication of the costing system. No matter how good the system is, however, there will always be a major proportion of overheads which cannot be identified with one department and therefore must be *apportioned*.

6.4 Cost Apportionment

The process of sharing overhead costs amongst two or more cost centres, in proportion to the estimated benefit they receive, is known as *cost apportionment*.

What constitutes a *fair basis* on which to apportion the overhead cost differs according to the nature of the overhead and the type of organisation; there are some methods which are widely accepted as equitable. A typical example is rent, where it is normal to share the total cost over the various cost centres on the basis of the *floor space* occupied. Depreciation may be apportioned on the basis of the *book value* of the plant and machinery.

6.5 Overhead Analysis

To charge overheads to cost centres a statement known as an **overhead analysis** is prepared. This shows the overheads by their *nature* (e.g., rent, rates, salaries) and the *total cost* of each one. The various cost centres are shown, and by a process of apportionment and allocation the individual overheads are charged to the cost centres.

The cost centres to which overheads are to be allocated and apportioned in the first instance are both production and service cost centres. Production cost centres are those where the cost units pass through that centre for work to be carried out on them. Service cost centres, such as the Maintenance Department, canteen and Stores, support the production cost centres, but no cost units pass through them. As all overheads are charged, finally, to the cost units, the total overheads of each of the service cost centres must be shared over the production cost centres. The overhead analysis ensures this in a straightforward and systematic way.

The *six* stages in constructing an overhead analysis are:

1. List overheads *vertically* by their nature – e.g., rent, salaries.
2. Show cost centres *horizontally* at the top of the page, both production cost centres and service cost centres.
3. *Allocate overheads* to those cost centres where the amounts and destinations are *known with certainty*.
4. Apportion the remaining overheads to all cost centres on the basis of the *estimated benefit* they receive.
5. *Total the overheads* for all of the cost centres.
6. *Allocate and apportion service cost centres* to production cost centres.

Example 6.1

The Rubton Co. has a factory with three departments: press shop, assembly shop and canteen. The overhead costs for a 12 month period are:

	£
Rent and rates	60,000
Heat and light	30,000
Repairs to plant and machinery	30,000
Depreciation of plant and machinery	15,000
Stock – fire insurance premium	15,000
Indirect material	2,500
Indirect wages	12,500
	14,800

The following additional information is available:

	Press shop	Assembly	Canteen
Area – square feet	1,500	1,000	500
No. of employees	10	15	5
Indirect wages	£3,000	£3,800	£8,000
Indirect materials	£5,000	£7,500	–
Value of plant	£120,000	£100,000	£80,000
Value of stocks	£75,000	£75,000	–

An overhead analysis must be constructed, the first figures being inserted are for those overheads which can be allocated to the cost centres – in this case, indirect wages and indirect materials. The other overheads are then apportioned on the basis shown in Figure 6.1.

In some instances, it may be possible to argue for a different basis of apportionment than that used in Figure 6.1, although the method shown would appear to be 'fair'.

Fig 6.1 *Overhead analysis*

Overhead	Basis	Total	Press	Assembly	Canteen
		£	£	£	£
Indirect materials	Alloc	12,500	5,000	7,500	
Indirect labour	Alloc	14,800	3,000	3,800	8,000
Rent	Area	60,000	30,000	20,000	10,000
Heat/light	Area	30,000	15,000	10,000	5,000
Repairs	Value of plant	30,000	12,000	10,000	8,000
Deprectn	Value of plant	15,000	6,000	5,000	4,000
Salaries	Number Empls	15,000	5,000	7,500	2,500
Insurance	Value	2,500	1,250	1,250	–
			77,250	65,050	37,500
Canteen	Number Empls		15,000	22,500	(37,500)
		179,800	92,250	87,550	–

Notes

1. To apportion the overheads the total figure must be *shared in proportion* over the three departments. For example, *rent* is shared on the basis of *area*, so the £60,000 is divided by the total area of 3,000 sq ft area, and the charge per sq ft is multiplied by the space occupied by each department. For the press shop, this is £20 x 1,500 sq ft.
2. The overheads for the *canteen* have been apportioned by sharing the total of £37,500 in proportion to the *number of employees in the production departments*, 10:15.

Having allocated and apportioned all the overheads to each of the cost centres, the *canteen overheads* must be *apportioned to the production cost centres*. This has been done on the basis of the *number of employees in the production cost centres*, ignoring those employed in the canteen. This method may be contentious as not all employees will use the canteen, but it is almost certain that the canteen employees themselves will eat there. In the absence of further information, which may be costly to collect, the method used is acceptable because of its simplicity. If a more sophisticated basis is required, there are a number of more rigorous methods to apportion the costs of service cost centres which are examined in the next section.

6.6 Service Cost Centres

In most companies, there are a number of service cost centres (such as maintenance and stores) supporting the production cost centres. The overheads for these service departments must be apportioned to the production cost centres so that a *full charge* for all overheads incurred by the company can be made to the cost units. The basis for apportionment should be as fair as possible, but possible bases are:

Basis of apportionment	*Service cost centre*
No. of employees	Canteen, Personnel Dept
Material requisitions	Stores
Maintenance labour hours	Maintenance Dept

Before the service departments' costs can be apportioned, the *total departmental costs* must be calculated. There are three different forms of relationship which can take place between service departments and/or production departments. Each form of these relationships requires a different accounting treatment.

6.6.1 Service to production departments only

This is where the service department carries out work *only for production departments*, and no other service department receives any benefit. Even in the simplest organisation this form of relationship is unlikely to arise, but you may find such a question in an examination. In such an event, the total service department costs are spread over the production departments on a fair basis of apportionment.

6.6.2 Service departments working for other service departments

In this case, one service department provides a service for other departments, both production and service, but it is a *one way relationship* – the original service department does not get reciprocal support from the other service departments. For example, in an organisation with two service departments in addition to production cost centres, Service Department A may be providing a service to Service Department B as well as Production Departments, but B does not provide a service to A. In this instance, the costs of Service Department A are apportioned first, to ensure that Service Department B bears a part of its fair share of all overheads. The total cost of Service Department B is then shared over the production cost centres as in Example 6.2.

Example 6.2

A company has two production departments and two service departments. Service Department A provides services for Service Department B, but the latter gives support only to the production departments. The overheads for both service departments are to be apportioned equally over the departments enjoying their services. An overhead analysis has been completed to arrive at the total overheads for each of the four departments.

	Production Dept 1 £	Production Dept 2 £	Service Dept A £	Service Dept B £
Total overheads	10,000	20,000	3,000	2,000
Secondary apportionment				
Service Dept A	1,000	1,000	(3,000)	1,000
Subtotal	11,000	21,000	–	3,000
Service Dept B	1,500	1,500	–	(3,000)
Production Dept overheads				
Total	12,500	22,500	–	–

6.6.3 Reciprocal services

Where two or more service departments provide services for each other as well as for the production departments, this is known as *reciprocal services*. The total cost of one Service Department cannot be found until the charge for the second Service Department is calculated. But the charge for the second Service Department is *not known* until a share of the overheads from the first Service Department has been apportioned to it. There are a number of ways of dealing with this apparently insoluble problem and we will consider them by looking at the simplest first.

6.6.3.1 Elimination method

Using this method, the cost effects of the reciprocal services are *ignored*. A specified order of apportioning each department's overheads is used, normally taking the department with the largest overheads first, and no return charge is made from other departments.

This makes the process very simple. It can be argued that the method does lead to inaccuracies and should not be used; however, the process of apportionment is only arbitrary and, unless significant differences are going to arise, this method is acceptable.

In the elimination method the Service Department with the largest cost is normally apportioned first and thus eliminated from all future calculations. The remaining service departments are then apportioned in a similar manner. Some examination questions may give a specified order for closing the service departments, and you should adhere to this.

Example 6.3

Data for apportionment of service department overheads

	Service depts		Production depts	
	No. 1	No. 2	No. 3	No. 4
Proportion for apportioning Service Dept 1	–	10%	40%	50%
Proportion for apportioning Service Dept 2	20%	–	40%	40%
	£	£	£	£
Overhead costs	5,000	3,000	18,000	16,000
Apportionment of Service Dept 1	(5,000)	500	2,000	2,500
Apportionment of Service Dept 2	–	(3,500)	1,750	1,750
Total	–	–	21,750	20,250

Note that the final apportionment of the total overheads for Service Department 2 is to the production departments only in the *ratio to the benefits they receive*.

6.6.3.2 Repeated distribution or continuous allotment method
In this method, the appropriate proportion of the costs of the first service department are apportioned to the second service department, then the costs of this department are apportioned to all the other departments, including the first service department. This process of reapportioning the overheads continues until the amount remaining in any one service department is insignificant. Example 6.4 uses the same figures as in the elimination method explained in Example 6.3.

Example 6.4

	Service depts		Production depts	
	No. 1 £	No. 2 £	No. 3 £	No. 4 £
Overhead costs	5,000	3,000	18,000	16,000
Apportion Service Dept 1	(5,000)	500	2,000	2,500
Subtotal	–	3,500	20,000	18,500
Apportion Service Dept 2	700	(3,500)	1,400	1,400
Subtotal	700	–	21,400	19,900
Apportion Service Dept 1	(700)	70	280	350
Subtotal	–	70	21,680	20,250
Apportion Service Dept 2	14	(70)	28	28
Subtotal	14	–	21,708	20,278
Apportion Service Dept 1	(14)	–	7	7
Total	–	–	21,715	20,285

Notes

1. The total overheads for the two production departments (£21,715 and £20,285) is the same as the commencing figure of overhead for the four departments (£42,000).
2. The first apportionment of service department overheads can be done in any order; it will make no difference to the final result.
3. When the repeated reapportionment reduces the service department overheads to insignificant amounts, they can be rounded up.

6.6.3.3 Algebraic method
In this method, an equation must be constructed for each Service Department to show the total overhead costs for that department, including its share of other service department overheads. The same data is used as in Examples 6.3 and 6.4.

Let a = total overheads for SD1 when SD2 has been apportioned
Let b = total overheads for SD2 when SD1 has been apportioned
Therefore a = £5,000 + 0.20b
    and b = £3,000 + 0.10a

This data can be rearranged to obtain the following equations:

$$a - 0.20b = £5,000$$
$$b - 0.10a = £3,000$$

The value of either a or b must be calculated by converting one of them to the *same value*, and thus cancelling from the equations. This can be done by multiplying the first equation by 5 and adding the results:

$$
\begin{aligned}
5a - b &= £25,000 \\
b - 0.10a &= £3,000 \\
\hline
4.9a &= £28,000 \\
a &= £28,000 \\
\hline
&\quad 4.9 \\
a &= £5,714
\end{aligned}
$$

This result can be used to complete the overhead apportionment.

Example 6.5

	Service depts		Production depts	
	No. 1 £	No. 2 £	No. 3 £	No. 4 £
Overhead costs	5,000	3,000	18,000	16,000
Apportion Service Dept 1	(5,714)	571	2,286	2,857
Subtotal	(714)	3,571	20,286	18,857
Apportion Service Dept 2	714	(3,571)	1,428	1,429
Total	–	–	21,714	20,286

Notes on the three methods

The repeated distribution method and the algebraic method give approximately the same results, although sometimes there may be a small discrepancy.

Examination questions should make it clear as to which method is to be applied. If in doubt, fall back on the safest maxim for students, which is to *use the method that you know best!*

Exercises

1. Explain what is meant by:

(**a**) Cost allocation.
(**b**) Cost apportionment.

2. What are the stages in constructing an overhead analysis?

3. Describe the THREE methods whereby Service Department overheads can be apportioned when there are reciprocal services.

4. Construct an overhead analysis from the following data to find the total overheads of the two production departments. Use the elimination method to apportion the service departments overheads.

Overheads for period

	£
Rent	1,600
Heat and light	160
Machine depreciation	2,000
Machine insurance	80
Indirect materials	100
Indirect labour	400

	Stores	Maintenance	Production depts	
			No. 1	*No. 2*
Area (sq metres)	50	150	300	300
Machine value	–	£5,000	£20,000	£15,000
Indirect materials	£20	£20	£30	£30
Indirect labour	£50	£50	£200	£100
Apportion				
Maintenance	10%		40%	50%
Stores			50%	50%

5. *SP*

SP plc is engaged mainly in retailing fashion and leisure wear, camping equipment and protective clothing. The company's head office and warehouse are located on the east coast and the 50 shops it operates are divided into three divisions as follows:

Division	No. of shops
North-west	16
West	13
South	21

Servicing of the shops is undertaken from the head office for:

* personnel and staff training;
* window display, sales promotion and advertising;
* warehousing and distribution – no goods are delivered direct to the shops from the manufacturers.

Costs for the three service functions are budgeted for the next financial year, as shown below, and it is desired to determine methods of apportioning these costs to the three retailing divisions.

	Personnel and staff training	Window display, sales promotion and advertising	Warehousing and distribution
	£000	£000	£000
Wages	40	65	140
Transport	9	30	115
Other costs	8	135	30

Other information available from the budget for the next financial year is as follows:

	North-west	West	South	Total
	£000	£000	£000	£000
Sales	2,760	2,320	4,120	9,200
Cost of goods sold	1,154	978	1,668	3,800
Branch wages	422	358	645	1,425
Divisional administration	45	45	53	143

You are required to:
(a) prepare a statement showing how you would apportion the costs of the service functions to each of the retailing divisions;
(b) explain, in a brief report, why you have selected the bases of apportionment that you have used in (a) above, and state any limitations.

(CIMA, May 1986)

6. *Factory*
(a) In a factory with four Production Departments and two Service Departments, the operating costs for the month of October were as shown below. The cost of running the canteen is apportioned to each department on the basis of the estimated use of the canteen by the employees in each department. Similarly, the cost of the boiler house is apportioned on the basis of the estimated consumption of power used by each department.

Costs for October were:	£
Production Department: 1	200,000
2	500,000
3	300,000
4	400,000
Service Department: Canteen	50,000
Boiler house	100,000
Total	1,550,000

The Service Department costs are apportioned as follows:

	Canteen	Boiler house
	%	%
Production Department: 1	10	20
2	30	10
3	20	30
4	30	20
Service Department: Canteen	–	20
Boiler house	10	–
	100	100

You are required to prepare a cost statement showing the costs of operating the four Production Departments after the costs of the Service Departments have been reapportioned to each Production Department.
(b) Comment briefly on the problems associated with apportioning Service Department costs to Production Departments.

(CIMA, November 1982)

7 Overheads – Absorption

7.1 Introduction

Chapter 6 looked at methods for collecting overheads to the production departments, but two problems remain. First, a suitable method for charging the overheads to the *individual cost units* passing through the production departments must be found. This leads to the solution to the second problem – calculating the *total cost* of a particular job or an individual item.

The method of charging overheads to cost units – that is, overhead absorption or overhead recovery – is of great importance when the products are not similar and yet pass through the same production departments. In the course of manufacture these dissimilar cost units make a differing demand on the production resources for unequal lengths of time. The amount of overhead charged to the individual cost unit should reflect these differing demands made upon the production resources.

A method must be found to charge a fair proportion of the overhead to the cost unit. This is done by calculating the **overhead absorption rate**. It is found by taking the overhead for a particular cost centre and dividing it by the *number of units of the absorption base*. It is important to note that the units of the absorption base need not be the same as the cost units; there are a variety of units of the absorption base, as explained in the next section.

7.2 Bases of Absorption

If all cost units were identical, production cost centre overhead could be divided by the number of cost units to share it fairly. Often in practice, however there is a problem of dissimilar cost units and a way must be found of absorbing or recovering the overhead into the various cost units to reflect the demands made by each cost unit on the production facilities. Because companies differ in the nature of their production and the sophistication of their record keeping, there are a number of absorption rates and the most appropriate one must be selected. The various bases of absorption are shown using the following data:

Production Department 1 for the month of January

Total cost centre overhead (TCCO)	£10,000
No. of cost units	1,000
Direct labour hours	2,500
Machine hours	500
Direct wages	£5,000
Direct materials	£2,000
Prime cost	£7,000

1. *Cost unit overhead absorption rate*

$$\frac{\text{TCCO}}{\text{No. of cost units}} = \frac{£10,000}{1,000} = £10 \text{ overhead per unit}$$

Advantages: Easy and very accurate.
Disadvantages: Cost units must be identical or capable of conversion.

2. *Direct labour hour overhead absorption rate*

$$\frac{\text{TCCO}}{\text{No. of labour hours}} = \frac{£10,000}{2,500} = £4 \text{ overhead per direct labour hour (DLH)}$$

Advantages: There is a direct relationship between the passage of time and the overhead cost which is reflected in this base. The method can be used with incentive scheme payments and additional statistics can be made readily available for other costing purposes.
Disadvantages: Records must be maintained and greater clerical work is required.

3. *Machine hour overhead absorption rate*

$$\frac{\text{TCCO}}{\text{No. of machine hours}} = \frac{£10,000}{500} = £10 \text{ overhead per machine hour}$$

Advantages: There is a direct relationship between the passage of time and the overhead cost, and this base should be used when machine hours predominate in the cost centre.
Disadvantages: Records must be maintained and greater clerical work is required.

4. *Direct wage percentage overhead absorption rate*

$$\frac{\text{TCCO}}{\text{Direct Wages}} = \frac{£10,000}{£5,000} = \begin{array}{l}\text{200\% of direct wage cost} \\ \text{or £2 overhead charge for} \\ \text{every £1 of direct wages}\end{array}$$

Advantages: Quick and easy to apply.
Disadvantages: Workers' rates of pay and speeds of operation may vary, and no account is taken of this.

5. *Material cost percentage overhead absorption rate*

$$\frac{\text{TCCO}}{\text{Direct materials}} = \frac{£10,000}{£2,000} = \begin{array}{l}\text{500\% of material cost or} \\ \text{£5 overhead charge for} \\ \text{every £1 of direct material}\end{array}$$

Advantages: Quick and easy to apply.
Disadvantages: No element of time is taken into account and if two jobs take the same time, but one contains more expensive materials, the overhead charge will differ.

6. *Prime cost percentage overhead absorption rate*

$$\frac{\text{TCCO}}{\text{Prime cost}} = \frac{£10,000}{£7,000} = \begin{array}{l}\text{143\% of prime cost or £1.43} \\ \text{overhead for every} \\ \text{£1 of prime cost.}\end{array}$$

Advantage: Quick and easy to apply.
Disadvantages: Compounds disadvantages of methods 4 and 5 above.

7.3 Application of Rates

Having demonstrated the calculation of the different bases of absorption, these principles can be applied to an example of a particular job carried out by a company. The job passes through one only Production Department and the total factory cost of the job must be calculated from the information given.

Example 7.1

Job No. 633

Direct material cost	£50
Direct wages paid (£2 per hour)	£30
Time taken on machine	10 hours

Production Department information for period

No. of direct labour hours	4,000
No. of machine hours	3,000
Direct wages paid	£8,000
Direct materials	£6,000
No. of cost units	500
Total overheads for period	£12,000

The first step is to calculate the *overhead absorption rate*. For purposes of explanation, each of the units of base discussed previously are used:

1. Cost unit overhead absorption rate

$$\frac{£12,000}{500} = £24 \text{ for each cost unit}$$

2. Direct labour hour overhead absorption rate

$$\frac{£12,000}{4,000} = \begin{array}{l}£3 \text{ overhead for each direct labour, and as} \\ 15 \text{ hours were worked on the job the total} \\ \text{overhead charge will be £45}\end{array}$$

3. Machine hour overhead absorption rate

$$\frac{£12,000}{3,000} = \begin{array}{l}£4 \text{ overhead for each machine hour, and as} \\ 10 \text{ hours were worked on the job the total} \\ \text{overhead charge will be £40}\end{array}$$

4. Direct wage percentage overhead absorption rate

$$\frac{£12,000}{£8,000} = \begin{array}{l}150\% \text{ of direct wage cost, and as this is £30} \\ \text{the overhead charge will be £45}\end{array}$$

5. Direct material percentage overhead absorption rate

$$\frac{£12,000}{£6,000} = \begin{array}{l}200\% \text{ of direct material cost, and as this is} \\ £50 \text{ the overhead charge will be £100}\end{array}$$

6. Prime cost percentage overhead absorption rate

$$\frac{£12,000}{14000} = \begin{array}{l}85\% \text{ of prime cost, and this is £80 the} \\ \text{overhead charge will be £68}\end{array}$$

The next step is to apply one of the overhead absorption rates to Job No. 633, to calculate the total cost. Before charging overheads to the job the costs are:

Job No. 633

	£
Material cost	50
Wage cost	30
Prime cost	80

If the cost unit overhead absorption rate is used, the charge for overheads will be £24, giving a total cost for the job of £104. If, however, the direct material overhead absorption rate is used the total cost for the job would be £180. Depending on which rate is adopted a different total cost is found. Which is the right one?

The answer is that they are *all theoretically right*, but the company must decide which particular overhead absorption rate it will consistently adopt. Where the information is available, it is best to select a rate which is *related to some aspect of time*. In this example, direct labour hours or machine hours could be selected. As more labour hours are available in the Production Department for the period than machine hours, it would appear that the company incurs the overhead primarily to provide labour. Using the direct labour hour overhead absorption rate, the total cost is:

Job No. 633

	£
Material cost	50
Wages	30
Prime cost	80
Overhead	45
Total cost	125

Having selected a particular rate for one department the company should consistently apply this unless there is a revision of policy. It is perfectly normal to have different bases of absorption in different departments; for example, in the same company the machine hour overhead absorption rate may be used in the Machine Shop and a direct labour hour rate in the Assembly Department.

In unsophisticated costing systems, a 'blanket' or factory wide overhead absorption rate may be used. Overheads will not be compiled for each separate department and the standard rate will be applied, irrespective of the department through which the cost unit passes. This makes for considerable ease in application and a saving in clerical work. However, there is a considerable loss in accuracy because the overheads charged to the product do not normally represent fairly the *resources drawn from the different departments*. Students are not recommended to use a blanket rate.

7.4 **Predetermined Overhead Rates**

In the previous section it was implied that overhead absorption rates were based on actual costs. In practice, it is normal to use *predetermined rates*: in other words, prior to the start of an accounting period the budgeted overheads are determined and the budgeted units of base. This allows a predetermined rate to be calculated at the beginning of a period and applied throughout.

There are two reasons for not using actual figures. First, the collection, analysis and absorption of overheads to products or jobs takes a considerable time. The figures may not be finalised until the end of the financial year and clearly it is not possible to wait until the actual figures are known before invoicing customers, submitting estimates and generally carrying out the management function. Secondly, if the industry is seasonal, short term fluctuations in activity will be smoothed out by using predetermined rates.

7.5 **Under or Over Absorption**

Because predetermined rates are used, it is highly unlikely that the actual overheads for the period will be the same as those charged to the production process on the predetermined basis. The difference can be because the actual overheads are not the same as the budget, or because the amount of the base of absorption differs from the budget, or a combination of these two factors.

If the overheads charged to production are higher than the actual overheads for the period, this is referred to as *over absorption* (i.e., too much overhead has been charged). When the overheads absorbed into production are lower than the actual figures it is known as *under absorption*.

Example 7.2

Cost centre X: Period 2

	Budget	Actual
Overheads	£12,000	£11,642
Direct labour hours	4,000	3,700

$$\text{Direct labour hour overhead absorption rate} = \frac{£12,000}{4,000} = £3 \text{ per hour}$$

The overheads absorbed into production are calculated at £3 per hour multiplied by the actual activity:

Overhead absorbed = £3 × 3,700 hours = £11,100
Actual overheads incurred   £11,642

Under absorption   £542

The final profit for the period can be ascertained only by adjusting the figures by the amount of overhead under absorbed. Assuming the figures as shown below, the under absorption would be treated as follows:

Cost centre X: Period 2

	£
Direct materials	8,000
Direct labour	10,000
Absorbed overheads	11,100
Calculated production cost	29,100
Overheads under absorbed	542
Total production cost to Profit & Loss Account	29,642

The under or over absorption of overheads is known only when the actual production and actual overheads for a period have been calculated. Although under or over absorbed overheads must finally be brought into the calculation of the profit figure, a Suspense Account may be opened to transfer the periodic adjustments.

7.6 Non-production Overheads

The examples used so far have concentrated on production overheads – those indirect costs associated with the factory. Part of the total cost of a product is made up by *non-production overheads*, such as administration and selling costs. Although these may be substantial, many companies do not follow the same procedures for absorbing these indirect costs as with production overheads. Different methods are used and the guiding principle is to remain *consistent*. Possible treatments for these overheads are now considered.

7.6.1 Administration overheads
If possible, it is best to apportion administration overheads between production and selling *before* the allocation and apportionment of production overheads to cost centres. These apportioned administrative

costs can then be incorporated into the selling and production overheads and be absorbed or computed in the usual way.

7.6.2 Selling overheads

These cannot be added to the cost of a product until the product is *actually sold*. The overheads can normally be absorbed on a valuation basis; factory cost is a good measure. The selling overhead absorption rate (SOAR) can be calculated as a percentage to be added to the factory cost as follows:

$$\text{SOAR} = \frac{\text{Total selling overheads}}{\text{Total factory cost of sales}}$$

Exercises

1. What is a 'blanket' or factory wide overhead absorption rate, and what are its disadvantages?
2. Describe three different overhead absorption rates, and their respective disadvantages and disadvantages.
3. What are the arguments in favour of using predetermined overhead absorption rates?
4. Kensington plc has two departments and the budget for the year is:

	Dept A	Dept B
Overhead costs	£96,000	£150,000
Direct labour hours	12,000	30,000
Machine hours	24,000	10,000

A job No. 241Z is accepted with the following direct costs:

	£
Direct materials	300
Direct wages:	
Dept A 20 hours at £2.50 per hour	50
Dept B 50 hours at £2.50 per hour	125

In Dept A 20 machine hours will be required for the job, but none will be required in Dept B.
Calculate the appropriate overhead absorption rates and the total cost of the job.

5. Write a short essay on the subject 'Overhead Absorption', paying particular attention to:

(a) the meaning of the expression;
(b) the basic information required;
(c) the methods commonly used; and
(d) the problems which arise in practice.

(ACCA, December 1976)

6. A light engineering company calculates its production overhead absorption rate at the end of each month by dividing the total actual overheads incurred by the total number of units produced in that month. This blanket absorption rate is then applied retrospectively to the month's production.

A variety of products are manufactured by the company and total demand is such that there are some unavoidable seasonal fluctuations in production activity. Production departments vary from light assembly work to semi-automatic machine shops and within each department the processing time for different products varies considerably, in some cases products do not pass through every department.

Required:
Critically examine the effect of the above system of overhead absorption on the company's product costs, pricing policy and consequent profitability.

(ACCA, June 1979)

7. Bookdon Plc manufactures three products in two production departments, a Machine Shop and a Fitting Section; it also has two Service Departments, a canteen and a machine maintenance section. Shown below are next year's budgeted production data and manufacturing costs for the company.

Product	X	Y	Z
Production (units)	4,200	6,900	1,700
Prime cost:			
Direct materials (£ per unit)	11	14	17
Direct labour –			
Machine shop (£ per unit)	6	4	2
Fitting section (£ per unit)	12	3	21
Machine hours (per unit)	6	3	4

Budgeted overheads	Machine shop	Fitting section	Canteen	Machine maint-enance section	Total
	£	£	£	£	£
Allocated overheads	27,660	19,470	16,600	26,650	90,380
Rent, rates, heat and light					17,000
Depreciation and insurance of equipment					25,000
Additional data:					
Gross book value of equipment	150,000	75,000	30,000	45,000	
No. of employees	18	14	4	4	
Floor space occupied – sq metres	3,600	1,400	1,000	800	

It has been estimated that approximately 70% of the Machine Maintenance Section's costs are incurred servicing the Machine Shop, and the remainder incurred servicing the Fitting Section.

Required:

(a) (i) Calculate the following budgeted overhead absorption rates:
A machine hour rate for the Machine Shop.
A rate expressed as a percentage of direct wages for the Fitting Section.
All workings and assumptions should be clearly shown.
(ii) Calculate the budgeted manufacturing overhead cost per unit of Product X.

(b) The production director of Bookdon Plc has suggested that, 'as the actual overheads incurred and units produced are usually different from that budgeted and as a consequence profits at each month end are distorted by under/over absorbed overheads, it would be more accurate to calculate the actual overhead cost per unit each month end by dividing the total number of all units actually produced during the month into the actual overheads incurred.'

Critically examine the production director's suggestion.

(ACCA, June 1982)

8. SM Ltd makes two products, Exe and Wye. For product costing purposes a single cost centre overhead rate of £3.40 per hour is used based on budgeted production overhead of £680,000 and 200,000 budgeted hours as shown below.

	Budgeted overhead £	Budgeted hours
Department 1	480,000	100,000
Department 2	200,000	100,000
	680,000	200,000

The number of hours required to manufacture each of the products is:

	Exe	Wye
Department 1	8	4
Department 2	2	6
	10	10

There were no work in progress or finished goods stocks at the beginning of the period of operations but at the end of the period 10,000 finished units of Exe and 5,000 finished units of Wye were in stock. There was no closing work in progress.

The prime cost per unit of Exe is £30. The pricing policy is to add 50% to the production cost to cover administration, selling and distribution costs and to provide what is thought to be a reasonable profit.

You are required to:
(a) calculate what the effect is on the company's profit for the period, by using a single cost centre overhead rate compared with using departmental overhead rates;
(b) show by means of a comparative statement what the price of Exe would be using:
  (i) single cost centre overhead rate; and
  (ii) departmental overhead rates;
(c) discuss briefly whether the company should change its present policy on overhead absorption, stating reasons to support your conclusion.

(CIMA, May 1984)

9. A company is preparing its production overhead budgets and determining the apportionment of these overheads to products.

Cost centre expenses and related information have been budgeted as follows:

	Total	Machine Shop A	Machine Shop B	Assembly	Canteen	Main-tenance
Indirect wages (£)	78,560	8,586	9,190	15,674	29,650	15,460
Consumable materials (incl. maintenance) (£)	16,900	6,400	8,700	1,200	600	–
Rent and rates (£)	16,700					
Buildings insurance (£)	2,400					
Power (£)	8,600					
Heat and light (£)	3,400					
Depreciation of machinery (£)	40,200					
Area (sq ft)	45,000	10,000	12,000	15,000	6,000	2,000
Value of machinery (£)	402,000	201,000	179,000	22,000	–	–
Power usage – technical estimates (%)	100	55	40	3	–	2
Direct labour (hours)	35,000	8,000	6,200	20,800	–	–
Machine usage (hours)	25,200	7,200	18,000	–	–	–

Required:
(a) Determine budgeted overhead absorption rates for each of the production departments, using bases of apportionment and absorption which you consider most appropriate from the information provided.

(**b**) On the assumption that actual activity was:

	Machine Shop A	Machine Shop B	Assembly
Direct labour hours	8,200	6,500	21,900
Machine usage hours	7,300	18,700	–

and total production overhead expenditure was £176,533, prepare the production overhead control account for the year (you are to assume that the company has a separate cost accounting system).

(**c**) Explain the meaning of the word 'control' in the title of the account prepared in answer to (b).

(*ACCA, June 1986*)

8 Job and Batch Costing

8.1 Introduction

Job costing is the method used when work is carried out according to the customer's special requirements. The 'job' is a cost unit consisting of a *single order* or *contract*. Usually each job is for only a short time and is carried out on the company's premises; small jobs may be carried out on the premises of the client. The job keeps its identity as a separate unit, although it may go through various stages.

A *separate record is opened* as each job is ordered, and used to maintain the costing details of the job. To ensure that all costs for each job are recorded properly, there must be a good system of production control, works documentation and labour recording.

The purpose of job costing is to establish the profit or loss for each separate job. The records maintained serve also for estimating the costs of *future jobs* and *setting the price to be quoted to customers*. For jobs which are incomplete at the end of an accounting period, job costing provides a work in progress valuation for the balance sheet.

Batch costing is used when a quantity of identical items are manufactured *as a batch*. This could be either because a customer orders a quantity of identical items, or because replacement stock is required and an internal manufacturing order has been raised.

Costing a batch is very similar to costing a job and the same procedures are followed, treating the batch as a separate, identifiable job. The costs are collected in the same way as for job costing. When the batch has been completed, the total batch cost is divided by the number of good units produced, giving the *cost per unit*.

8.2 Job Costing Procedure

The type of job costing adopted depends on the complexity of the organisation and the sophistication of its recording system. In any form of job costing, *rigorous costing procedures* must be present in the organisation; the main stages are:

1. The customer informs the company of the *specific requirements*.
2. The Estimating Department prepares an *estimate* quoting a selling price to the customer.
3. If the customer accepts the estimate and places an order, a *works order* with an identifying number is raised.
4. A *materials requisition note* is prepared so that materials can be drawn from stores.
5. A *purchase requisition* is sent to the Buying Department for any special materials and equipment which may be required.
6. A *job card* showing the various stages of the work to be performed is raised.
7. A *labour requirement note* is sent to Personnel Department if workers with special skills are required.
8. The job is entered into the *production schedule* to fix a starting date which will allow completion by the agreed delivery date.

8.3 Collection of Job Costs

It is essential that a company maintains adequate records to collect the costs *relevant to a specific job*. Failure to do so means that the actual profit or loss for the job cannot be calculated and future estimates based on past records will be incorrect. All the different systems for collecting job costs concentrate on identifying the materials and labour for each job, and recording these on a job cost card or job cost sheet.

Job costing is usually combined with *absorption costing*, and the examples in this chapter are based on that assumption. A simple system for collecting costs has the following characteristics:

1. A *material requisition note* is sent to the stores identifying the materials required for the job. The materials requisition note is used to cost the materials to the job cost sheet.
2. A *job ticket* is given to the worker who is performing the first operation. The starting and finishing times for that operation are clocked on the ticket, the same procedure being followed for subsequent operations. Finally, the job ticket is sent to the cost office where the time is costed and entered on the job cost sheet.
3. *Direct expenses* are entered on the job cost sheet from invoices or an analysis of the cash book.
4. The *cost of materials and direct labour* as recorded on the job cost sheet is charged to the job account.
5. The job account is charged with an appropriate share of the *factory overheads*, usually on the basis of predetermined overhead absorption rates.

6. If a job is incomplete at the end of an accounting period, it should be valued at *factory cost* on the balance sheet.
7. On completion of the job, an appropriate share of the administration, selling and distribution overheads are charged to the job account. This account now shows the *total cost* of the job.
8. The difference between the total cost of the job and the agreed selling price represents the *profit* or *loss* on the job.
9. In a company which has a number of very small jobs, it is not practicable to have a separate job cost sheet for each one. Instead a *general jobbing account* is kept, to which all the costs for the jobs are charged.

8.4 Job Cost Cards or Job Cost Sheets

These are the *key documents* in a job costing system. The specimen job cost card in Figure 8.1 below would be used for relatively small jobs; for larger jobs only the summary figures would be entered on the job card from an analysis schedule.

8.5 Calculating the Cost of a Job

All the various stages in job costing have now been explained and can be applied in a simple example of costing a particular job. If the company is operating absorption costing, it is important to work out the predetermined overhead rates and to include a share of the overheads in the cost of the job.

Example 8.1

The following information refers to a company in the jobbing industry using absorption costing:

Department	Budgeted overheads £	Absorption base
Machine shop	12,000	3,000 machine hours
Press shop	7,000	2,000 labour hours
Assembly department	6,000	2,500 labour hours

Administration and selling overheads are calculated at 25% of factory cost.

JOB COST CARD

Customer .... Delivery date ....
Job No .... Start date ....
Job description .... Order No ....
Invoice price .... Despatch note No ....

MATERIALS					DIRECT WAGES				DIRECT EXPENSES			OVERHEADS		
Date	R. Note	Qty	Price	Cost	Date	Hours	Rate	Cost	Date	Ref	Cost	Unit of Base	Rate	Cost

SUMMARY   £   p

Direct materials
Direct wages
Direct expenses   ————

Prime cost
Factory overhead   ————

Factory cost
Admin & selling
  overhead   ————

Total cost
INVOICE PRICE   ————

PROFIT   ————

Fig 8.1 *Job cost card*

An order has been placed for Job No. A24 with a selling price of £5,200. The following information relates to that job:

Direct materials £1,415
Direct labour:
   Machine shop 50 hours at £3.00 per hour
   Press shop 180 hours at £2.50 per hour
   Assembly 100 hours at £1.75 per hour
   Time booked in the machine shop for the job is 210 machine hours

The first step in calculating the costs is to work out the *overhead absorption rates*:

Machine shop $\dfrac{£12,000}{3,000}$ = £4.00 per machine hour

Press shop $\dfrac{£7,000}{2,000}$ = £3.50 per labour hour

Assembly $\dfrac{£6,000}{2,500}$ = £2.40 per labour hour

Total Cost Job No. A24

	£	£
Direct materials		1,415
Direct wages – Machine shop	150	
Press shop	450	
Assembly	175	
		775
Prime cost		2,190
Factory overheads		
Machine shop (210 × £4.00)	840	
Press shop (180 × £3.50)	630	
Assembly (100 × £2.40)	240	
		1,710
Factory cost		3,900
Administration and selling overheads		975
Total cost		4,875
Profit		325
Selling price		5,200

Exercises

1. What are the main stages in job costing?
2. Describe what is meant by batch costing.

3. Draw up an example of a job cost card to be used for relatively small jobs.

4. A company has established the following annual budgets:

Factory	Total fixed overhead	£33,000
	Total direct labour hours	22,000
Dept A1	Total variable overhead	£18,000
	Total direct labour hours	9,000
Dept A2	Total variable overhead	£16,000
	Total direct labour hours	10,000

A job has been accepted which has the following direct costs:

Direct materials – 18 kilos at £5.10 per kilo
Direct wages – Dept A1 18 hours at £3.50 per hour
              Dept A2 32 hours at £3.00 per hour

What is the total cost of the job, and what is the profit as a percentage of costs if the selling price is £500?

5. *Process plant division*
The process plant division of a group of companies has built a food packaging machine to a customer's requirements. A price of £49,000 has been quoted with the intention of achieving a profit of 25% on the selling price.

Customer:	Bond Foods Ltd
Customer's order no.:	7206 dated 3 February 19X6
Job order no.:	1412
Date work started:	5 March 19X6
Date job completed in factory:	29 April 19X6
Date delivered:	2 May 19X6
Date commissioned:	6 May 19X6

	March £	*April* £
Materials used:		
Machining dept	2,900	700
Assembly dept	1,900	1,400
Direct wages rate per hour:		
Machine dept	4	4.40
Assembly dept	5	5.25
	Hours	*Hours*
Direct labour hours:		
Machining dept	200	100
Assembly dept	50	500
Machine hours in machining dept	350	180
Technical drawings (direct cost)	£2,115	

Production overhead is absorbed at the predetermined rate of £10 per direct labour hour in the assembly department and £15 per machine hour in the machining department.

Commissioning costs – i.e., installation and initial running-in of the machine at the customer's site – were £750 and these are to be treated as a direct production cost.

Selling and general administration costs are charged to jobs at the rate of $33\frac{1}{3}$ % of production cost.

You are required to prepare a job order cost sheet, and insert on it the information given above in such a way as to be useful to management.

(*CIMA, May 1986*)

6. In order to identify the costs incurred in carrying out a range of work to customer specification in its factory, a company has a job costing system. This system identifies costs directly with a job where this is possible and reasonable. In addition, production overhead costs are absorbed into the cost of jobs at the end of each month, at an actual rate per direct labour hour for each of the two production departments.

One of the jobs carried out in the factory during the month just ended was Job No. 123. The following information has been collected relating specifically to this job:

400 kilos of Material Y were issued from stores to Department A. 76 direct labour hours were worked in Department A at a basic wage of £4.50 per hour. 6 of these hours were classified as overtime at a premium of 50%.

300 kilos of Material Z were issued from stores to Department B. Department B returned 30 kilos of Material Z to the storeroom being excess to requirements for the job.

110 direct labour hours were worked in Department B at a basic wage of £4.00 per hour. 30 of these hours were classified as overtime at a premium of 50%. All overtime worked in Department B in the month is a result of the request of a customer for early completion of another job which had been originally scheduled for completion in the month following.

Department B discovered defects in some of the work, which was returned to Department A for rectification. 3 labour hours were worked in Department A on rectification (these are additional to the 76 direct labour hours in Department A noted above). Such rectification is regarded as a normal part of the work carried out generally in the department.

Department B damaged 5 kilos of Material Z which then had to be disposed of. Such losses of material are not expected to occur.

Total costs incurred during the month on all jobs in the two production departments were as follows:

	Dept A £	Dept B £
Direct materials issued from stores*	6,500	13,730
Direct materials returned to stores	135	275
Direct labour, at basic wage rate†	9,090	11,200
Indirect labour, at basic wage rate	2,420	2,960
Overtime premium	450	120
Lubricants and cleaning compounds	520	680
Maintenance	720	510
Other	1,200	2,150

Materials are priced at the end of each month on a weighted average basis. Relevant information of material stock movements during the month, for materials Y and Z is as follows:

	Material Y	Material Z
Opening stock	1,050 kilos	6,970 kilos
	(value £529.75)	(value £9,946.50)
Purchases	600 kilos at	16,000 kilos at
	£0.50 per kilo	£1.46 per kilo
	500 kilos at	
	£0.50 per kilo	
	400 kilos at	
	£0.52 per kilo	
Issues from stores	1,430 kilos	8,100 kilos
Returns to stores	–	30 kilos

* This includes, in Department B, the scrapped Material Z. This was the only material scrapped in the month.
† All direct labour in Department A is paid a basic wage of £4.50 per hour, and in Department B £4.00 per hour. Department A direct labour includes a total of 20 hours spent on rectification work.

Required:
(a) Prepare a list of the costs that should be assigned to Job No. 123. Provide an explanation of your treatment of each item.
(b) Discuss briefly how information concerning the cost of individual jobs can be used.

(ACCA, December 1985)

9 Contract Costing

9.1 Introduction

Contract costing is an application of job costing, but is used when the cost units are large and the time taken to complete them is long, frequently in excess of 12 months. Contract costing is widely used in the construction industry and civil engineering.

The *cost unit*, or *contract*, is normally completed away from the company's premises and the work may even be conducted abroad. The client company appoints a contractor and a formal contract is drawn up. This details the *work* to be carried out, the method and timing of *payments*, and any financial *penalties* which can be invoked if the work is not completed to the required standard and in the agreed time.

A company will have a number of contracts running at the same time. Contract costing allows the company to identify and collect the costs relevant to each contract, so that a profit or loss may be calculated for each of them. Certain procedures must be followed to assess correctly the costs relevant to each contract, and specific rules must be applied to calculate the profit (or loss) on a contract that remains unfinished at the end of a financial period.

9.2 Features of Contract Costing

Nine things are of particular concern:

1. The contract takes a *long time* to complete and may span more than one accounting period.
2. Most material is ordered *specifically for a particular contract*.
3. Most labour is *direct to that specific contract*, including staff such as site clerks and security guards whose salaries are normally regarded as indirect costs.
4. Most *expenses are direct*, for example, electricity meters will be fitted on site, and telephones, except in small contracts.
5. Some method must be found to charge plant and machinery to site; a *time basis* is usually the most appropriate.
6. Nearly all the overhead costs can be identified as *head office costs*.

7. An architect or surveyor inspects the work periodically and issues *certificates* to the contractor detailing satisfactorily completed work. These are valued at selling price and the contractor sends the certificate to the client with an invoice to obtain *interim payments*.
8. Frequently the formal contract states that the client can withhold a proportion of the contract value, for example 10%, for a certain period after the completion of the contract. These are known as **retention monies**, and during the period until the date when they are finally settled, the contractor must make good any defects appearing in the work carried out.
9. Because of the environmental conditions on site and the involvement of non-clerical staff, great attention must be paid to the *collection of prime documentation* and *control of costs*.

9.3 **Contract Costing Procedure**

Seven matters are crucial here.

1. A *separate account* for each contract is opened. This is charged with all the costs and credited with the contract price. Each contract account is regarded as a *separate profit and loss account*. The profits or losses on each of the separate accounts will be transferred to the main Profit and Loss on Contracts Account.
2. *Materials* are charged either direct from the invoice or, if drawn from stores, from a materials requisition note. Any materials returned to stores from site are credited to the contract.
3. All *labour* must be charged to each contract; if employees are working on a number of contracts at the same time, they must complete time sheets for each contract.
4. *Direct expenses* can be charged directly from invoices submitted to the company; in the construction industry, a significant amount of the work may be completed by subcontractors.
5. *Plant and machinery* may be charged to the contract in a number of ways depending on the circumstances:
   (a) If it is hired from a plant firm, the cost of the hire is a *direct expense*.
   (b) If it is owned by the company, short term usage may be charged at an *hourly rate for each item of plant*.
   (c) If owned and on site long term, the contract will be *charged* with the value of plant on arrival at site and *credited* with its depreciated value upon removal.

6. *Overhead costs* are usually added on the basis of a predetermined overhead rate. If a contract is unfinished at the end of the financial period, head office general costs are not added and only production overheads are included in the value of any work in progress.

7. The *contract price* is credited to the Contract Account from the architect's certificate and any profit or loss transferred to the Profit and Loss on Contracts Account. An agreed percentage should not be transferred until all defects have been remedied and retention monies received. On uncompleted contracts at the end of the financial period, only a proportion of the profit should be transferred; this is dealt with in section 9.5.

9.4 Completed Contracts

If a contract is completed during the accounting period there are few problems. Example 9.1 considers the example of a block of flats completed for a client in the financial year, and the period for retention monies having been satisfied.

9.5 Uncompleted Contracts

When a contract has not been completed at the end of the year, two problems arise. First, the *value of work in progress* must be correctly shown in the contract account and in the balance sheet. Secondly, a conservative estimate of *profit on the contract to date* must be calculated.

Example 9.1

Contract 866
Chilton Flats

	£
Value of materials delivered to site	230,000
Wages	250,000
Subcontractors' charges	30,000
Site expenses	20,000
Plant transferred to site	160,000
Materials returned to store	30,000
Plant removed from site (depreciated value)	124,000
Head office charges (10% of wages)	25,000
Value of work certified	750,000

Contract account 866

	£		£
Materials	230,000	Materials to store	30,000
Wages	250,000	Plant transferred	124,000
Plant to site	160,000	Cost of contract cd	561,000
Subcontractors	30,000		
Site expenses	20,000		
Head office charges	25,000		
	715,000		715,000
Cost of contract bd	561,000	Value of work	750,000
Profit on contract	189,000	certified	
	750,000		750,000

The profit on the contract of £189,000 will be transferred to the main Profit and Loss Account. The value of the work certified of £750,000 will be debited to the Client's Account and this is shown as a debtor in the balance sheet until payment has been received.

When work has been done, but has not yet been certified, it is *valued at cost* without any profit element.

The calculation of the profit is laid down in Statement of Standard Accounting Practice 9, and students are advised to study this in full. Essentially, the estimated profit for the entire contract is first calculated by deducting the total estimated costs of the contract from the total value of the contract. The total estimated costs of the contract comprise the costs incurred to date, the estimated costs to completion and the estimated future costs of any rectification and guarantee work. The amount of profit to be taken in the financial period is then calculated by applying the following formula:

$$\text{Profit to date} = \frac{\text{Cost of work completed}}{\text{Total estimated costs of contract}} \times \frac{\text{Estimated}}{\text{contract profit}}$$

If it is calculated that by deducting the total estimated costs from the value of the contract there is a *loss* and not a profit, the loss should be shown in full in the accounts for the period.

Example 9.2

The following is an example of a contract for the construction of a new shopping precinct.

Contract 211
Bunden Shopping Precinct

	£
Materials purchased for contract	125,160
Materials from stores	22,240
Operating costs of plant and machinery	11,470
Book value of plant to site 1 January	96,420
Wages	43,120
Subcontractors' charges	20,000
Site salaries	10,000
Site expenses	16,200
Materials returned to stores	1,230
Book value of plant transferred from site	10,640
Materials on site at 31 December	10,020
Book value of plant on site at 31 December	74,240
Cost of work in progress not certified at 31 December	32,580
Total contract value	500,000
Work certified by architect at 31 December	250,000
Estimated costs to complete contract	220,000

Contract 211 account

	£		£
Materials purchased	125,160	Material to stores	1,230
Materials from stores	22,240	Plant transferred	10,640
Plant operating costs	11,470	Materials on site cd	10,020
Plant to site	96,420	Plant on site cd	74,240
Wages	43,120	WIP cd	32,580
Subcontractors' costs	20,000	Cost of work certified	215,900
Site salaries	10,000		
Site expenses	16,200		
	344,610		344,610
Cost of work certified bd	215,900	Value of work certified	250,000
Profit on contract to date	16,718		
Profit in suspense cd	17,382		
	250,000		250,000
1 January			
Materials bd	10,020	Profit in suspense bd	17,382
Plant bd	74,240		
WIP bd	32,580		

Notes

1. The cost of work certified of £215,900 is the net balance on the first part of the contract account.
2. The cost of work not certified being work in progress (WIP) of £32,580 is added to the cost of work certified to give the costs of all work done to date of £248,480.
3. The profit for the period is calculated as follows:

	£	£
Contract value		500,000
Costs to date	248,480	
Estimated future costs	220,000	468,000
Estimated total profit		31,520

$$\text{Profit for period} = \frac{£248,480}{£468,480} \times £31,520$$

$$= £16,718$$

4. The profit in suspense is calculated as follows:

	£
Value of work certified	250,000
Less costs of work certified	215,900
	34,100
Less profit in period	16,718
Profit in suspense	17,382

9.6 Statement of Standard Accounting Practice 9

SSAP 9 is being reviewed and, in November 1986, Exposure Draft 40 (ED40) was issued which proposed a change in the definition of a long term contract and a different accounting treatment. The main principle is that *turnover* and *profit* should be reflected in the profit and loss account annually over the life of the contract, with exceptions for contracts where the outcome cannot reasonably be assessed before completion.

A *long term contract* is one which is for the manufacture or building of a single substantial entity or the provision of a service where the time taken falls into different accounting periods and is normally expected to extend for a period *exceeding one year*.

Long term contracts should be classified separately under *stocks*. The amount is the cost incurred after deducting foreseeable losses and applicable payments on account. Separate disclosure is proposed of net costs *less* foreseeable losses and applicable payments on account. The amount by which recorded turnover exceeds payments on account should be separately disclosed in debtors under the heading 'amounts recoverable on contracts'.

Exercises

1. What are the main features of contract costing?
2. What is meant by:
   (a) an architect's certificate;
   (b) retention monies?

3. Explain the different methods which can be used for charging plant and machinery to a contract.
4. Prepare a Contract Account based on the following information as at 31 December 19X7:

Contract 2267
Commencement date 1 January 19X7

	£
Contract price	550,000
Materials delivered to site	42,220
Wages	68,880
Site expenses	16,250
Value of plant on 1 January	250,000
Materials on site at 31 December	3,850
Work certified	210,000
Cost of work completed but uncertified	10,500
Estimated costs of completion	286,250
Plant is depreciated at 20% per annum	

5. Jigantic Ltd is a building company engaged in the construction of hospitals and other major public buildings; most of the contracts undertaken extend over a three or four year period.

   Shown below are the expenses incurred for the year ended 31 May 1981, together with other operating details, for three of the contracts in which the company is currently engaged.

	Contract A £000	Contract B £000	Contract C £000
Contract price	4,000	10,200	12,000
Value of work certified by contractees' architects	2,350	7,500	11,000
Cash received from contractees	2,000	6,750	9,900
Work in progress at 1.6.1980	–	2,400	6,700
Costs incurred during the year:			
Materials	1,100	1,600	1,050
Labour	700	1,150	975
Other expenses, excluding depreciation	350	475	775
Plant and equipment:			
Written down value at 1.6.1980	300	800	700
Written down value at 30.5.1981	600	525	175
Purchases during the year	725	400	125
Cost of work not yet certified	75	–	800

The agreed retention rate is 10% of the value of work certified by the contractees' architects.

Contract C is nearing completion and the site manager estimates that costs, additional to those tabulated above, of £425,000 will be incurred in order to complete the contract. He also considers that the plant and equipment on site will be worthless by the time the contract is complete.

The nature of the work undertaken by Jigantic Ltd is such that it may be regarded as reasonable for the company to include in its annual accounts a prudent estimate for profit attributable to that part of the work on each contract certified as complete at the end of each accounting year.

The opening stock of work in progress shown above includes an estimated profit of £1,150,000 for Contract C, but none for Contract B as, at the beginning of the year, work on this project had only recently commenced.

The directors of Jigantic Ltd propose to incorporate into the company's Profit and Loss Account for the year ended 31 May 1981, the following amounts of profit/(loss) for each contract:

Contract A	Nil
Contract B	£720,000
Contract C	£2,400,000

Required:
(a) Making whatever calculations you consider necessary, carefully explain whether you agree with the proposed profit/(loss) figures for the above contracts. If you consider any of the proposed amounts are

inappropriate suggest, with supporting explanations and calculations a more suitable figure.

(b) Show the relevant entries for each contract, incorporating any revised profit/(loss) figures, on the balance sheet of Jigantic Ltd as at 31 May 1981.

(ACCA, June 1981)

6. One of the building contracts currently engaged in by a construction company commenced 15 months ago and remains unfinished. The following information relating to work on the contract has been prepared for the year just ended.

	£000
Contract price	2,100
Value of work certified at end of year	1,840
Cost of work not yet certified	35
Costs incurred:	
Opening balances	
Cost of work completed	250
Materials on site (physical stock)	10
During the year	
Materials delivered to site	512
Wages	487
Hire of plant	96
Other expenses	74
Closing balance	
Materials on site (physical stock)	18

As soon as materials are delivered to the site, they are charged to the Contract Account. A record is also kept of materials as they are actually used on the contract. Periodically a stock check is made and any discrepancy between book stock and physical stock is transferred to a General Contract Materials Discrepancy Account. This is absorbed back into each contract, currently at a rate of 0.4% of materials booked. The stock check at the end of the year revealed a stock shortage of £4,000.

In addition to the direct charges listed above, general overheads of the company are charged to contracts at 5% of the value of work certified. General overheads of £13,000 had been absorbed into the cost of work completed at the beginning of the year.

It has been estimated that further costs to complete the contract will be £215,000. This estimate includes the cost of materials on site at the end of the year just finished, and also a provision for rectification.

Required:
(a) Explain briefly the distinguishing features of contract costing.
(b) Determine the profitability of the above contract, and recommend how much profit (to the nearest £000) should be taken for the year just ended. (Provide a detailed schedule of costs.)

(c) State how your recommendation in (b) would be affected if the contract price was £3,500,000 (rather than £2,100,000) and if no estimate has been made of costs to completion.

(ACCA, June 1987)

10 Continuous Operation Costing

10.1 Introduction

Continuous operation costing is used where the goods or services being costed are the result of continuous or repetitive operations or processes. Costs for a financial period are collected for the particular operation or process and divided by the number of units produced in the period to give an *average cost per unit*.

There are three forms of continuous operation costing: *output costing, service costing,* and *process costing*. The first two methods are dealt with in this chapter and process costing is dealt with in Chapter 11.

10.2 Output Costing

Output costing can be used where the company is manufacturing *only one product*, or basically one product, although it may be manufactured in a number of grades or types. Output costing is often used in highly mechanised industries, such as quarrying and cement manufacturing.

Because there is only one product, this is a very simple form of costing. Costs are collected for a financial period, usually by nature, and the total divided by the number of units produced to give an *average cost per unit*. There may be partly completed units at the end of a financial period, but these are usually ignored. The reason for this somewhat cavalier attitude is that the partly completed units are often insignificant in number compared to total production, and the numbers tend to be constant at the end of each period, thus minimising any effect.

The cost statements used by companies vary according to the nature of the industry and the information needs of managers. To allow some control, it is normal to show the costs classified by their nature for the period and to calculate the cost per unit. It is advantageous to give some *basis of comparison*, and this may be the results for the previous period or budgeted figures. Example 10.1 uses the cost unit of one kilo of the material being produced.

Example 10.1

Unit cost statement for January
(Total units produced 10,000)

Item of cost	Cost	Cost per kilo	
		Actual	Budget
	£	£	£
Wages and salaries	25,000	2.50	2.55
Materials	40,000	4.00	4.02
Packaging	2,000	0.20	0.21
Transport	3,500	0.35	0.33
Depreciation	4,500	0.45	0.45
Electricity	8,000	0.80	0.75
Rates and rent	7,500	0.75	0.75
Repairs and maintenance	1,500	0.15	0.12
Total cost	92,000	9.20	9.18

10.3 Service Costing

Service costing is used when it is desired to cost *specific services* or *functions*. These may be referred to as service centres, departments or functions. The services may be offered to external parties, such as hotel accommodation and car hire, or the company may be a manufacturing organisation which needs to know the cost of services provided internally – e.g., stores, maintenance department and canteen.

The major difficulty with service costing is in *identifying a cost unit* accurately to measure the service being provided. A hotel may decide the cost unit is an occupied bed night; a transport company may select a passenger-mile – that is, the cost of carrying one passenger for one mile. If a particular industry can agree a common cost unit *inter-company comparisons* are possible.

As many of the companies using service costing are substantial organisations operating on a national basis, rigorous systems and procedures are required for the collection and analysis of costs. The organisations are often subject to fluctuating demands for their services – for example, in a bus company where there are certain peak periods of demand during the day. This fluctuating activity means that managers will need information to distinguish between those costs which are fixed and those which are variable. The treatment of these costs is examined in Chapter 13 Marginal Costing.

Not all service organisations use service costing. This is because the services provided by the company are not sufficiently identical, and so a form of *job costing* is used. Architects and accountants are good examples of organisations offering different services to each of their clients and therefore using job costing.

Service costing has a number of features. Normally the cost of direct materials is relatively small compared to direct labour and overhead costs. The service may not be a revenue earner so the purpose of service costing is not to establish a profit or loss, but to provide information to managers for *cost control* and the *prediction of future costs*.

A simple example of service costing in operation is in a canteen where meals are being provided to employees. The company needs to know the costs of running the canteen and the average cost per meal. A monthly statement is drawn up showing the various costs which may comprise:

(a) *Labour costs*   Hourly paid staff need to complete *time sheets* to provide this information and the salaries of any supervision (e.g., canteen manager's salary) are regarded as fixed costs.
(b) *Food and drink*   These costs are collected from *invoices*. A separate stores may be in operation for food and drink supplies which will require the usual controls and procedures.
(c) *Consumables*   These are such items as crockery, cutlery and cleaning materials which all require regular renewal.
(d) *Ovens and furniture*   A *depreciation charge* is made for these fixed assets.
(e) *Occupancy or building costs*   Some apportionment is made so that the canteen carries a fair share of the costs incurred through the *space* it occupies.

All the above costs are recorded for the month to give a total cost figure for running the canteen. By dividing this figure by the number of meals served during the period, the average cost per meal can be calculated.

11 Process Costing

11.1 Introduction

In some industries production follows a number of *distinct but successive stages*. The finished output at one stage of production becomes the input for the next stage. At the end of all the stages, or processes, the completed production is sold or transferred to finished goods stock. Examples of this type of production are chemical works, oil refineries and paint manufacturers.

Process costing is used in companies with this type of production to find the cost of the product at each of the various stages or processes of manufacture. For each process both direct costs (such as materials and labour) and manufacturing overheads are charged. By dividing the costs of one process by the number of units, the *average cost per unit* is calculated.

Cost units which are similar in nature pass through each of the production processes. It is essential that *appropriate cost units* are chosen. Where the product is liquid, the cost unit might be a litre; with a solid product, a kilogram or tonne would be more appropriate.

As cost units move from the first process to the second, the costs incurred to date are *transferred with them*. This cost transfer carries through all the processes and the costs thus accumulated give the total cost at the end of production. Figure 11.1 overleaf illustrates how the costs follow the production flow on a cumulative basis.

Figure 11.1 illustrates the general principle of process costing whereby the costs of one process are transferred to the next process, where additional costs are incurred, until the units are transferred to the finished goods stock. The actual method of process costing used varies from one company to another. However, there are certain characteristics which are common to all process costing systems:

1. There are *separate processes* which can be defined easily and the costs collected to them.
2. The *output* from one process forms the *input* of the following process.
3. Both *direct costs* and *overheads* are charged to the processes.

98

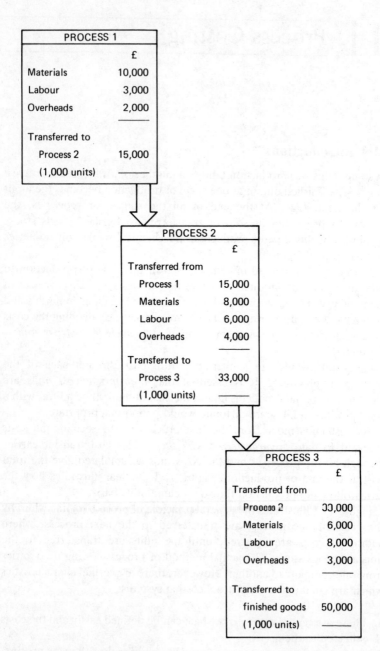

Fig 11.1 *The build up of costs*

4. *Costs are accumulated* in respect of cost units as production goes through the various processes.
5. The total cost of a process for a period of time, divided by the cost units for that period, gives an *average unit cost* of manufacture.

11.2 Equivalent Units

The last characteristic of a process costing system, identified above, was the calculation of the average cost unit; the formula for this is:

$$\text{Cost per unit (cpu)} = \frac{\text{Costs incurred during period}}{\text{No. of units produced}}$$

This formula has been applied to Example 11.1 to arrive at the average cost per unit for the period.

Example 11.1

Production for January – completed units	50,000
Direct material cost	£5,000
Direct labour cost	£3,500
Manufacturing overheads	£1,500

$$\text{Cost per unit} = \frac{£10,000}{50,000}$$

$$= £0.20$$

It would be unusual to have completed units only remaining at the end of a period; there would also be a number of units which were only part complete and these represent work in progress (WIP). The costs incurred during the period are for all the units, both the completed ones and those which are partly complete. To find out the average cost per unit for the total effective production, the partly completed units must be converted into their *equivalent number of fully completed units*. For example, if there are 2,000 partly completed units in work in progress, it may be decided they are 75% complete. The 2,000 partly completed units can be converted into their equivalent number of complete units, in this instance 1,500 (see Example 11.2). The formula for calculating the cost per unit when there is work in progress is:

$$\text{Cost per unit} = \frac{\text{Cost incurred during period}}{\text{Units completed} + \text{Equivalent units in WIP}}$$

Example 11.2

Production for January – completed	6,000 units
Work in progress	2,000 units
The work in progress is 50% complete	

	£
Direct material cost	4,000
Direct labour cost	2,800
Manufacturing overhead	1,600

$$\text{Cost per unit} = \frac{£8,400}{6,000 + (2,000 \times 50\%)}$$

$$= \frac{£8,400}{7,000}$$

$$= £1.20$$

11.3 Cost Elements

The costs incurred in production comprise the usual elements – i.e., materials, labour and overheads. When the work in progress – the partly completed units – is examined at the end of a period, the *degree of completion* may differ for each of the cost elements. The units may be almost complete as far as materials are concerned, but further substantial labour and overhead costs may be necessarily incurred to complete the units. In such a case, the cost elements must be treated separately to find out the number of equivalent units and to calculate the cost per unit, as in Example 11.3.

Example 11.3

Data for Process No. 1 for the month of January

	£
Direct material cost	8,050
Direct labour cost	12,375
Manufacturing overheads	8,400
5,000 fully completed units	
1,000 units in WIP	

The units in WIP are 75% complete for materials
50% complete for labour
25% complete for overheads

Cost element	Formula	Cost per unit £
Materials	$\dfrac{£8,050}{5,000 + (1,000 \times 75\%)}$	1.40
Labour	$\dfrac{£12,375}{5,000 + (1,000 \times 50\%)}$	2.25
Overheads	$\dfrac{£8,400}{5,000 + (1,000 \times 25\%)}$	1.60
Total cost per unit		5.25

Value of WIP (1,000 units)

		£	£
Materials	750 equivalent units @ £1.40	1,050	
Labour	500 equivalent units @ £2.25	1,125	
Overheads	250 equivalent units @£1.60	400	
			2,575
Value of completed units 5,000 @ £5.25			26,250
			28,825

The value of work in progress (£2,575), plus the value of the completed units (£26,250), adds up to the total cost incurred during January (£28,825). This is a check which should *always be carried out*.

So far, only one process has been considered. Let us take the above figure of 5,000 completed units at the end of January for Process 1 and add information concerning the next stage of manufacture, Process 2 in February (Example 11.4).

Example 11.4

Data for Process 2 in February:

Materials added at start of process	£6,000
Labour costs	£3,800
Overhead costs	£2,850
Completed units transferred to finished goods stock	4,500
Closing WIP (50% complete)	500

The value of closing WIP and completed production *transferred to finished goods* store at the end of February must be calculated. There are two points to watch here. First, Process 2 starts with the 5,000 units transferred from Process 1 at the end of January. Secondly, when calculating the number of equivalent units, there will be no further material costs incurred as materials were needed at the start of the process. Work in process is therefore 100 per cent complete as far as the material cost element.

To tackle Example 11.4 in a logical way, the information can be drawn up in the form of a table. The format shown in Table 11.1 can be used to solve most process costing questions.

Table 11.1 *Process 2 Costs for February*

Cost element	Total costs £	No. of completed units	Equivalent units in WIP	Total effective units	CPU* £	Value of WIP £
Previous process costs	26,250	4,500	500	5,000	5.25	2,625
Materials	6,000	4,500	500	5,000	1.20	600
Labour	3,800	4,500	250	4,750	0.80	200
Overheads	2,850	4,500	250	4,750	0.60	150
	38,900				7.85	3,575

	£
Value of completed units 4,500 @ £7.85	35,325
Value of WIP	3,575
	38,900

* CPU = cost per unit

Example 11.4 illustrates a number of important points. Columns 1 and 2 of Table 11.1 are straightforward; Column 3 shows the number of completed units transferred to finished goods stock. Column 4 gives the number of equivalent units in work in progress. There are 500 units in work in progress and for previous process costs and material costs the units are 100 per cent complete. (Previous process costs must be by definition *always complete*.)

The materials in Example 11.4 were added at the beginning of the process. This means that even when there are partly completed units in work in progress at the end of the period, the units must be complete as far as the material cost element is concerned. This is a favourite examination topic and the following rules should be applied:

1. If any cost elements are added at the start of the process, then *no further costs* of this nature will be incurred.
2. If any cost elements are added at the end of the process, as the units in work in progress have not reached this stage, *no part of the cost element* can be included in work in progress.
3. Having calculated the number of equivalent units, this is added to the number of completed units to give the number of *total effective units*. The total cost for each element in Column 2 is divided by the number of total effective units, giving the cost per unit in Column 6. To find the value of work in progress, the number of equivalent units in work in progress for each element is multiplied by the cost per unit.
4. The final stage is to calculate the value of the completed units at the bottom of Table 11.1, and add the value of work in progress to this figure. The total of these two figures *must agree* with the figure of total costs as shown in Column 2.

11.4 **Wastage**

Even with very efficient production processes there will be some wastage. Losses can arise due to liquids evaporating, or during the cutting and forming of metals, wood and other materials. Some of the losses are predictable and are regarded as normal, but even in a very efficient process errors sometimes occur, leading to unexpected losses. When the wastage is unexpected, it is regarded as *abnormal*.

Normal and abnormal wastage require different accounting treatments. If the level of wastage can be predicted, it is reasonable that the costs should be charged to the production itself. This has the effect of increasing the cost per unit of the good production. With abnormal losses, the costs must be excluded from the Process Account and charged to the Profit and Loss Account.

11.5 **Normal Wastage**

It is possible for losses to take place at any point in the process. Where wastage occurs part way through a process, some of the losses should be charged to work in progress. Where losses take place at the end of the process, possibly at a final inspection stage, only units fully completed during the period should be charged with the loss. The value of work in progress is not affected by the wastage.

The procedure for dealing with normal wastage occurring at the end of the process is:

1. Complete a table for *process costs*, as explained in section 11.3.
2. Column 3 of the table must show *all the completed units* – both the good units and those which form the normal losses.
3. Complete the table and use the cost per unit to calculate the value of the *normal wastage*.
4. Divide the value of the normal wastage by the number of good completed units and add to the original cost per unit to obtain a *revised cost per unit*.

Example 11.5

Materials (added at start of process)	£18,000
Labour costs	£31,350
Overheads	£15,725
Closing work in progress	2,000 units

The closing work in progress is 50 per cent complete labour and 25 per cent complete overheads. Total number of completed units is 18,000, of which 1,000 are scrapped. Now we can complete Table 11.2.

Table 11.2 *Table of processed costs – normal wastage*

Cost element	Total costs £	No. of completed units	Equivalent units in WIP	Total effective units	CPU* £	Value of WIP £
Materials	18,000	18,000	2,000	20,000	0.00	1,800
Labour	31,350	18,000	1,000	19,000	1.65	1,650
Overheads	15,725	18,000	500	18,500	0.85	425
	65,075				3.40	3,875

Value of normal wastage 1,000 units
@ £3.40 allocated to 17,000 good units   £3,400   0.20

                                          17,000

Revised cost per unit   3.60
Value of completed units 17,000 @ £3.60   £61,200
Value of work in progress   3,875

                                          £65,075

* CPU = cost per unit

11.6 **Abnormal Wastage**

Abnormal losses must be charged in full to the Profit and Loss Account. Abnormal losses are calculated by deducting normal losses from the total actual loss. If normal losses are 40 units, but the actual loss is 65 units, there will be abnormal losses of 25 units. (It is possible to have *abnormal gains* when the actual loss is lower than the normal loss.)

The abnormal losses must carry their share of the costs of the normal losses. It is important to do this calculation *before* working out the value of the abnormal losses to be charged to the profit and loss account. The procedure is:

1. Complete a table for *process costs*, as explained in section 11.3.
2. Column 3 of the table must show *all the completed units* – the good units, the normal losses and the abnormal losses.
3. Complete the table and use the cost per unit to calculate the value of *normal losses*.
4. Divide the value of normal losses by the total number of good units and abnormal loss units and add to the original cost per unit to obtain a *revised cost per unit*.
5. Multiply the revised cost per unit by the number of units of abnormal loss to obtain the *value of the abnormal loss* to be lcharged to the Profit and Loss Account.

Example 11.6

Material costs (added at start of process)	£50,000
Labour costs	£47,500
Overheads	£18,000
Closing WIP	2,000 units

The closing WIP is 75% complete labour and 50% complete overheads.

The total number of completed units is 8,000. Normal wastage is 500 units, but actual wastage in the period was 750 units.

Table 11.3 *Table of Process Costs – Abnormal Wastage*

Cost element	Total costs £	No. of completed units	Equivalent units in WIP	Total effective units	CPU* £	Value of WIP £
Materials	50,000	8,000	2,000	10,000	5.00	10,000
Labour	47,500	8,000	1,500	9,500	5.00	7,500
Overheads	18,000	8,000	1,000	9,000	2.00	2,000
	115,000				12.00	19,500

Value of normal wastage 500 units @ £12.00
  allocated to 7,500 remaining units = £6,000   0.80
                                    —————
                                      7,500
Revised cost per unit   12.80

                                                        £
Value of completed units 7,250 @ £12.80   92,800
Value of work in progress   19,500
Value of abnormal losses charged to
  Profit & Loss Account (250 @ £12.80)   3,200
                                                   ————————
                                                    115,500

* CPU = cost per unit

11.7 Work in Progress

Closing work in progress for a process at the end of one period forms the opening work in progress for the same process at the start of the next period. A problem of *valuation* therefore arises. Certain assumptions can be made to decide the method of valuation. We may assume that the units comprising work in progress are completed during the current period and use the First In, First Out method (FIFO). Alternatively, we can assume that the partly completed units forming the opening work in progress are mixed with the current period's production and as we do not know which units are completed at the end of the period, we can use the *average cost method* (see Example 11.7).

Example 11.7

A company has three processes; the details of the second process for a period are as follows:

> Value of opening work in progress 300 units (50% complete) £4,500
> Value of 900 complete units transferred from Process 1 at the start of the period £2,700
> Total costs for Process 2 for the period £8,100
> At the end of the period 1,000 complete units were transferred to Process 3
> The closing work in progress was 200 units (25% complete)

We will now calculate the value of closing work in progress using both methods.

1. *First In, First Out*

(a) No. of effective units produced by Process 2 during the period

	Units
Closing work in progress (200 × 25%)	50
Add completed units transferred to Process 3	1,000
	1,050
Less opening work in progress (300 × 50%)	150
Effective units manufactured in period	900

(b) Costs incurred in period to produce 900 effective units

	£
Transferred from Process 1	2,700
Other costs incurred in period	8,100
	10,800

(c) Valuation of closing work in progress

$$\frac{\text{Costs incurred in period (b)}}{\text{Number of effective units (a)}} = \frac{£10,800}{900}$$

$$= £12 \text{ per unit}$$

No. of equivalent units in closing work in progress (200 × 25%) = 50

Value of closing work in progress = 50 units @ £12
= £600

(d) Value of 1,000 completed units transferred to Process 3

	£
Value of opening work in progress	4,500
Costs transferred from Process 1	2,700
Other costs incurred in period	8,100
	15,300
Less value of closing work in progress	600
Value of completed units transferred to Process 3	14,700

2. *Average cost method.* In this method, the opening work in progress valuation plus the period costs are used to calculate the average cost per unit. The same average cost per unit is used to value both the closing work in progress and the completed units. Using the same data as for the First In, First Out method, the average cost method calculation is as follows:

(a) *Total number of effective units*   *Units*

Completed units transferred to Process 3	1,000
Add closing work in progress (200 × 25%)	50
	1,050

(b) *Total costs incurred*   £

Opening work in progress valuation	4,500
Costs transferred from Process 2	2,700
Costs incurred in period	8,100
Total costs incurred	15,300

(c) *Valuation of closing work in progress*

$$\text{Average cost per unit} = \frac{\text{Total costs incurred}}{\text{Total no. of effective units}}$$

$$= \frac{£15,300}{1,050}$$

$$= £14.5714$$

$$\text{Closing work in progress} = (200 \times 25\%) \times £14.5714$$
$$= £728.57$$

(d) *Valuation of 1,000 completed units transferred to Process 3*

	£
Transferred to Process 3 1,000 units @ £14.5714	14,571.40
Value of closing work in progress	728.57
Value of completed units transferred to Process 3	15,299.97

Exercises

1. What are the main characteristics of a process costing system?

2. Describe the two different methods for valuing closing work in progress.

3. Explain the different accounting treatments for normal and abnormal losses.

4. At the end of a period for a particular process the total costs incurred are: materials £20,000, labour £25,000, overheads £15,000. At the end of the period there are 12,000 completed units and 4,000 units in work in progress. The 4,000 units are 75% complete materials, 50% complete labour and 25% complete overheads. Calculate the value of the completed units and the work in progress.

5. (a) In the context of process costing, how would you distinguish a by-product from a joint product?

(b) Liquigas Ltd produces four products J, K, L and M through a process which for November 1976 cost £1,500,000. Production and sales during the month were as follows:

	Production	Sales	
	(tonnes)	(tonnes)	(per tonne)
J	5,000	4,000	£100
K	8,000	6,000	125
L	5,000	4,500	80
M	3,000	2,700	200

There were no stocks in hand at the beginning of November

You are required to prepare a statement showing the value of the stocks of the four products at the end of November and to state any assumptions you have made.

(ACCA, *December 1976*)

6. (a) Outline the characteristics and purpose of:
(i) Job costing;
(ii) Process costing.

(b) Explain carefully how material waste, or any other losses in production, should be treated in a process costing system, clearly indicating the reasons for your recommended treatment.

(ACCA, *December 1979*)

7. Everymans Foods Plc has recently acquired a factory which processes soya beans. The soya beans pass through a series of processes, including cleaning, roasting and grinding to a soya powder.

In the final process of the series, other ingredients are added to the powder and four distinct products emerge.

These are:

(i) Soya flour, which is bagged and sold to health food shops.
(ii) Soya broth soup, which is canned and sold to supermarkets.
(iii) Soya steak powder, which is passed through further operations to produce soya steak. The steak is then packed and sold to restaurants.
(iv) A small quantity of liquid which is sold to amateur gardeners as a fertiliser.

The management of Everymans Foods Plc require a process costing system to be installed, using monthly actual costs, and have requested your advice.

Required:
(a) Briefly explain the type of information which would be required in order to operate a process costing system in the above factory.
(a) Outline the type of information which would be produced by the above system and carefully explain the users and the limitations of that data.

(ACCA, December 1981)

12 Joint Product and By-product Costing

12.1 Introduction

By-product costing is used when a subsidiary or **by-product** is produced *in the course of manufacturing* the main product. The by-product is produced at the same time and from the same common process as the main product, although it may require further processing to make it marketable. The sales value of the by-product will be very low compared to the main product.

Joint product costing is used when *two or more products are produced from the same process*, using the same commonly processed materials up to their point of separation –i.e., the split off point. Each product has a significant sales value, but may require further processing after the split off point before it is marketable.

Joint and by-products are very common in industries such as the meat trade, oil refining, chemical works and mining. Because the definition of the terms depends on the *perceived significance of the sales value* of the products, companies will have differing views as to whether a product can be regarded as a joint or by-product. The processing of joint products is illustrated in Figure 12.1.

Fig 12.1   *The processing of joint products*

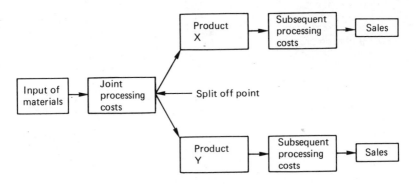

12.2 By-product Costing

By-products have a small sales value and there is little advantage in maintaining a complex costing system. It is usual to select a way of dealing with by-product costs which is simple, even if relatively insignificant problems are ignored. There are three ways of dealing with by-product costs:

1. No attempt is made to *distinguish* between the main product and the by-product. Any sales value from the by-product is added to the sales of the main product and all costs set against this to show the total profit. The view is taken that as there is a common process it is unrealistic, if not impossible, to attempt to attribute a proportion of the costs to the by-product.
2. If the sales value of the by-product is very small, it may be shown directly in the general Profit and Loss Account as 'Other income'. Any costs incurred after the split off point in bringing the by-product to a saleable condition are *deducted* from its income before showing in the Profit and Loss Account.
3. The preferred method is to *deduct the sales value* of the by-product *less any costs incurred after the split off point* from the total cost of production (see Example 12.1).

Example 12.1

Costs of production for period	£200,000
Opening stocks	Nil
Closing stocks of main product	5% of production
Sales revenue of main product	£220,000
By-product with net sales value of	£2,200
Subsequent costs of by-product	£200

	£	£
Sales of main product		200,000
Cost of production (£200,000 – £2,000)	198,000	
less closing stock (5%)	9,900	
Cost of sales		188,100
Profit		31,900

12.3 **Joint Products**

The joint costs incurred up to the split off point must be *apportioned* in some way. Subsequent costs, arising after the split off point, relate to each of the specific products and do not require apportionment. There are two methods which can be used to apportion the joint costs:

1. The physical units basis of apportionment can be applied to split the joint costs over the products in proportion to the *physical weight* or *volume* of the products.
2. The sales value basis apportions the joint costs in proportion to the *relative sales value* of the products.

Both these methods allow a closing value to be placed on the closing stocks of each of the joint products; both permit the costs and profits of each of the joint products to be determined; both provide information which management can use.

It must be borne in mind that one product *cannot be manufactured independently of the other*: the profit of one product is affected by the way the joint costs are apportioned.

12.4 **Physical Units Basis of Apportionment**

This method can be used only when the joint products separate after the split off point into *comparable states*. For example, this method cannot be applied if one product is a solid and the other a gas after the separation point. Additionally, if the products have very different sales values this is not reflected in the attributable profits and could lead to one product appearing to be very profitable and the other less so.

The method is simple to apply; the joint costs are simply apportioned on the basis of the output of each product to the total output measured by *weight* or *volume* (see Example 12.2).

Example 12.2

Joint processing costs	£6,000
Output of joint product X	2,000 kilos
Output of joint product Y	10,000 kilos
Sales value of product X	£1.10 per kilo
Sales value of product Y	£0.55 per kilo

	Product X	Product Y	Total
Output in kilos	2,000	10,000	12,000
	£	£	£
Sales	2,200	5,500	7,700
Apportioned costs	1,000	5,000	6,000
Profit	1,200	500	1,700
Profit/sales percentage	54.5%	9.1%	22.1%

By apportioning costs in proportion to output, Product X bears $\frac{2}{12}$ of the costs and thus has a profit/sales percentage of 54.5%.

12.5 Sales Value Basis of Apportionment

The advantage of this method is that it gives the *same profit/sales percentage for each product*. As managers often operate on an assumed relationship between costs and profits this method is widely used.

In applying this method, the joint costs are apportioned in the proportion that the *total sales value of each product* bears to the *total sales value for all output of the joint processes*. The selling price per unit is not used to apportion. Example 12.3 uses the same data as above.

Example 12.3

	Product X	Product Y	Total
	£	£	£
Sales	2,200	5,500	7,700
Apportioned costs	1,714	4,286	6,000
Profit	486	1,214	1,700
Profit/sales percentage	22.1%	22.1%	22.1%

The apportioned costs for Product X are calculated as follows:

$$\text{Product X costs} = \frac{£2,200}{£7,700} \times £6,000 = £1,714$$

Whichever method is used, the total profit remains the same, but the profit per product can be significantly different.

There are some products which incur further costs after the split off point to put them into a saleable condition. This means that there is no sales value at split off point which can be used as a basis for apportioning costs. If it is not possible to determine what the relative sales value should be at the split off point then the subsequent processing costs should be deducted from the final sales value to give a *notional sales value at split off point*. The notional sales value is then used to apportion costs in the way described.

Exercises

1. Describe the three different ways which may be used to deal with by-product costs.
2. What are the two methods used for apportioning joint costs?
3. The total joint cost of a process is £1,800. This gives an output of 700 kilos of Product X and 300 kilos of Product Y. The selling price of Product X is £2.40 per kilo and of Product Y £2.60 per kilo. Apportion the joint costs by using the physical units base and calculate the profit/sales percentage.
4. Using the same data as in question 3, apply the sales value basis of apportionment to these joint costs.
5. (a) Explain briefly the term 'joint products' in the context of process costing.
   (b) Discuss whether, and if so how, joint process costs should be shared amongst joint products. (Assume that no further processing is required after the split off point.)
   (c) Explain briefly the concept of 'equivalent units' in process costing.

(ACCA, June 1987)

6. Furnival has a distillation plant that produces three joint products, P, Q and R, in the proportions, 10:5:5. After the split off point the products can be sold for industrial use or they can be taken to the mixing plant for blending and refining. The latter procedure is normally followed.

For a typical week, in which all the output is processed in the mixing plant, the following Profit and Loss Account can be prepared:

	Product P	Product Q	Product R
Sales (volume)	1,000 gals	500 gals	500 gals
Price per gal	£12.50	£20	£10
Sales revenue	£12,500	£10,000	£5,000
Joint process cost (apportioned using output volume)	£5,000	£2,500	£2,500
Mixing plant Process costs	£3,000	£3,000	£3,000
Other separable costs	£2,000	£500	£500
	£10,000	£6,000	£6,000
Profit/(Loss)	£2,500	£4,000	(£1,000)

The joint process costs are 25% fixed and 75% variable, whereas the mixing plant costs are 10% fixed and 90% variable and all the 'other separable costs' are variable.

If the products had been sold at the split-off point the selling price per gallon would have been:

	Product P	Product Q	Product R
	£5.00	£6.00	£1.50

There are only 45 hours available per week in the mixing plant. Typically 30 hours are taken up with the processing of products P, Q and R (10 hours for each product line) and 15 hours are used for other work that generates (on average) a profit of £200 per hour after being charged with a proportionate share of the plant's costs (including fixed costs). The manager of the mixing plant considers that he could sell all the plant's processing time externally at a price that would provide this rate of profit.

It has been suggested:

(i) that, since product R regularly makes a loss, it should be sold off at the split-off point.
(ii) that it might be possible advantageously to change the mix of products achieved in the distillation plant. It is possible to change the output proportions to 7:8:5 at a cost of £1 for each additional gallon of Q produced by the distillation plant.

You are required to compare the costs and benefits for each of the above proposals. Use your analysis, to suggest any improvements that seem profitable and set out the weekly Profit and Loss Account for the improved plan, in a manner which you consider will assist the management with further problems of this type.

(ACCA, June 1985)

7. The marketing director of your company has expressed concern about Product X which for some time has shown a loss, and has stated that some action will have to be taken.

Product X is produced from Material A which is one of two raw materials jointly produced by passing chemicals through a process.

Representative data for the process is as follows:

Output	– Material A	10,000 kilos
	– Material B	30,000 kilos

Process costs	– Raw material	£83,600
	– Conversion costs	£58,000

Joint costs are apportioned to the two raw materials according to the weight of output.

Production costs incurred in converting Material A into Product X are £1.80 per kilo of Material A used. A yield of 90% is achieved. Product X is sold for £5.60 per kilo. Material B is sold without further processing for £6.00 per kilo.

Required:
(a) Calculate the profit/(loss) per kilo of Product X and Material B respectively.
(b) Comment upon the marketing director's concern, advising him whether you consider any action should be taken.
(c) Demonstrate for Product X, and comment briefly upon, an alternative method of cost apportionment.

(ACCA, December 1986)

8. *Distillation plant*
   A distillation plant, which works continuously, processes 1,000 tonnes of raw material each day. The raw material costs £4 per tonne and the plant operating costs per day are £2,600. From the input of raw material the following output is produced:

	%
Distillate X	40
Distillate Y	30
Distillate Z	20
By-product B	10

From the initial distillation process, distillate X passes through a heat process which costs £1,500 per day and becomes product X which requires blending before sale.

Distillate Y goes through a second distillation process costing £3,300 per day and produces 75% of product Y and 25% of product X1.

Distillate Z goes through a second distillation process costing £2,400 per day and produces 60% of product Z and 40% of product X2.

The three streams of products X, X1 and X2 are blended, at a cost of £1,155 per day, to become the saleable final product XXX.

There is no loss of material from any of the processes.

By-product B is sold for £3 per tonne and the proceeds are credited to the process from which the by-product is derived.

Joint costs are apportioned on a physical unit basis.

You are required to:
(a) draw a flow chart, flowing from left to right, to show for one day of production the flow of material and the build-up of the operating costs for each product;
(b) present a statement for management showing for each of the products XXX, Y and Z the output for one day, the total cost and the unit cost per tonne;
(c) suggest an alternative method for the treatment of the income receivable for by-product B than that followed in this question (figures are not required).

(CIMA, May 1987)

13 Marginal Costing

13.1 Introduction

Chapter 7 examined absorption costing which is a method of charging all costs to the product. Although this is the basis of all financial accounting statements, the information provided by absorption costing can be misleading when management is making decisions in certain circumstances. Example 13.1 illustrates this.

Example 13.1

Imagine I have a business supplying handmade rocking chairs. The selling price of each chair is £100 and the market is such that I can sell 5 chairs in one week. The timber for the chairs costs £20 per chair and I pay a craftsman £40 for each chair he makes. I rent a small showroom for £150 per week. What is my weekly profit?

Profit statement for 1 week (5 chairs)

	£	£
Sales		500
Materials	100	
Wages	200	
Rent	150	450
Profit		50

This statement includes all the costs and gives me a total profit figure. As I have sold 5 chairs the profit for each chair, based on the above information, is £10. But what if I make and sell only 3 chairs in one particular week; what will my profit be then? Using the information that the profit for one chair is £10, I may conclude that the profit for the week will be £30. The following profit statement gives a very different picture.

Profit statement for 1 week (3 chairs)

	£	£
Sales		300
Materials	60	
Wages	120	
Rent	150	330
Loss		(30)

From Example 13.1, it is easy to appreciate how a loss was made on 3 chairs instead of the anticipated profit, of £30. The rent of £150 remains the same each week *irrespective of the number of chairs made and sold*. The rent is known as a *fixed cost*, which is not influenced by changes in the level of activity. However, direct wages and material costs vary in proportion to changes in the level of activity.

It is this difference in the way that some costs vary with changes in the level of activity and some costs remain fixed which is the basis underlying *marginal costing*. By differentiating between fixed and variable costs management can be given information for planning and decision making.

13.2 Marginal Costing Definitions

Marginal costing has very few technical terms, but it is important to understand them in context in order to answer questions correctly. The key terms are:

1. *Variable costs* – those costs which, in total, tend to *follow the level of activity in the short term*. As activity increases, measured possibly by production or sales levels, so variable costs increase in total. As activity decreases, so variable costs decrease in total.
2. *Fixed costs* are those costs which, in total, tend to remain the same, *irrespective of changes in the level of activity in the short term*. For example, the rent of the factory or the salary bill is unlikely to change solely because the level of activity has temporarily changed in one week.
3. *Contribution* is the difference between the *sales value and the variable costs incurred in achieving those sales*; the contribution can be calculated for one unit or for any chosen level of sales. A complete understanding of what is meant by the term 'contribution' is essential.
4. *Marginal costing* is the application of the principle that *only variable costs are charged to the cost units*. The fixed costs for a particular period must be written off against the total contribution for that period to arrive at the profit or loss for the period.

A **marginal cost** is regarded by the accountant as the average variable cost and is assumed to be *constant* in the short term. Accountants tend to use the terms 'marginal cost' and 'variable cost' interchangeably, but some argue that it is preferable to adhere to the term 'variable cost'.

13 3 Examples of Fixed and Variable Costs

It is important to note that in the definitions of fixed and variable costs the words 'in total' are used. The variable cost per unit remains constant, but the total variable cost increases as activity increases. In Example 13.1, the material cost per chair is £20. This is a *variable cost* because as the number of chairs made increases or decreases so the total material cost changes. Figure 13.1 shows what happens to costs (known as *cost behaviour*) when activity increases.

Whether a specific type of cost is fixed or variable depends on the particular circumstances. A prime example is *direct wages*, sometimes termed operatives' wages. Accountants normally deem wages to be a variable cost in the absence of information to the contrary. However, fone can think of companies where activity may decrease for a short period, but the wages bill is not reduced in any way because the workforce is retained until business picks up. Unless there is information indicating an alternative treatment, the list of common costs in Figure 13.2 indicates how they should be regarded.

Some costs do not change in total in direct relationship to changes in the level of activity, neither do they remain fixed. Such costs are known

---

Fig 13.1   *Cost changes when activity changes*

	ACTIVITY INCREASES	ACTIVITY DECREASES
FIXED COSTS		
In total	Unchanged	Unchanged
Per unit	Decreases	Increases
VARIABLE COSTS		
In total	Increases	Decreases
Per unit	Unchanged	Unchanged

Nature	Nature of cost	Fixed	Variable
	Rent	X	
	Direct materials		X
	Direct labour		X
	Advertising	X	
	Salesmen's commission		X
	Depreciation	X	
	Metered power supply		X
	Warehouse wages	X	
	Machine operators' wages		X
	Rates	X	
	Lubricants	X	
	Accountants' salaries	X˙	

Fig 13.2   *Identifying fixed and variable costs*

as **semi-variable costs** as they contain both fixed and variable cost elements. To deal with semi-variable costs the fixed cost element must be identified and added to other fixed costs, and the variable cost element added to other variable costs. There are a number of methods for separating the fixed and variable elements; Example 13.2 illustrates the simplest.

Example 13.2

The first step is to identify the *total semi-variable costs for two different levels of production,* as in the following data;

Production level	Semi-variable costs
Units	£
6,000	8,000
16,000	13,000

The increase in units of 10,000 has brought about an increase in costs of £5,000. This increase in costs is due entirely to changes in the variable cost element as fixed costs do not change in total. The variable cost per unit is therefore

$$\frac{£5,000}{10,000} = £0.50 \text{ per unit}$$

The variable costs can now be calculated for each level of activity and deducted from the total semi-variable cost to give the *total fixed cost* (which should be *the same* at the different activity levels):

Production level	Semi-variable costs	Variable costs	Fixed costs
Units	£	£	£
6,000	8,000	3,000	5,000
16,000	13,000	8,000	5,000

13.4 Contribution

The contribution per unit is calculated by deducting the unit marginal cost from the unit selling price. The total contribution is calculated by deducting the total variable costs from the total sales.

Contribution is not profit because no regard has been paid to the fixed costs of the organisation. The contribution can be considered as a contribution to the fixed costs of the organisation and, when these have been completely covered, to profit. Unless a particular activity gives a contribution – i.e., the selling price is higher than the variable costs – that activity will never make a profit because the fixed costs still have to be borne.

With knowledge of the contribution per unit from any activity, it is simple to calculate the profit for a company, as in Example 13.3.

Example 13.3

A company manufactures an item with variable costs of £1.60 per unit and a selling price lof £2.20 per unit. In January it manufactures 2,000 units and the fixed costs for the month amount to £900. What is the profit for the month?

	£
Selling price per unit	2.20
Variable costs per unit	1.60
Contribution per unit	0.60

	£
Total contribution for January (2,000 units × £0.60)	1,200
Total fixed costs for January	900
Profit for January	300

13.4.1   Profit volume (or contribution sales) ratio

As sales and contribution are always in *direct proportion* to each other, a ratio can be calculated by expressing the contribution as a percentage of sales. This ratio is used in subsequent sections on decision making, but at the simplest level the contribution for a product can be quickly calculated at any given level of sales by using the ratio.

Example 13.4

In Example 13.3 the contribution was 60p per unit and the selling price was £2.20 per unit. The **profit/volume (P/V) ratio** is:

$$\frac{\text{Contribution}}{\text{Selling price}} = \frac{£0.60}{£2.20} \times 100 = 27.27\%$$

The contribution at any given level of sales can be found by using the formula:

Contribution = Sales × P/V ratio

So, in Example 13.4 the sale of 2,000 units at £2.20 each gives a contribution of £4,400 × 27.27% = £1,200.

13.5 Marginal Cost Statements

When drawing up information in the form of a marginal costing layout it is useful to show not only the total level of activity for the period, but also the figures per unit as demonstrated in Example 13.5.

Example 13.5

The KT Co manufactures an article with a selling price of £10.00 per unit. The variable costs per unit are £3.00 for direct materials, £2.00 for direct materials, £2.00 for direct labour and £2.00 for variable overheads. In the month of January sales are 4,000 units and the fixed costs are £10,000 for the month. Construct a marginal costing statement.

KT Co

Marginal costing statement
for the month of January

	Total production (4,000 units)		Figures for 1 unit	
	£	£	£	£
Sales		40,000		10
Variable costs:				
Direct materials	12,000		3	
Direct labour	8,000		2	
Overheads	8,000	28,000	2	7
Contribution		12,000		3
Total fixed costs		10,000		
Total profit		2,000		

From the figures for one unit you can calculate that the P/V ratio is 30%, so the total contribution with sales of £40,000 is £12,000, as shown on the marginal costing statement.

13.6 Uses of Marginal Costing

Marginal costing is most useful for a variety of short-term decision making, particularly where there are *changes in the level of activity*. The following types of business decisions can be helped by the application of marginal costing principles:

1. Setting the *selling price* of products, particularly in times of trade depression and when introducing new products.
2. Determining whether it is preferable to *manufacture* a component or to *buy it* from another company.
3. The proposed *closure or temporary cessation* of part of the business activities.
4. The acceptance of a *special order or contract*.
5. The comparison of *different methods* of manufacture.

Because of the immense value of the information supplied to management by marginal costing, its use is more widespread than the above list indicates. It is used by companies operating a flexible budgetary control system; it may underpin medium and long term corporate planning; it is the basis of **cost–volume–profit (C–V–P)** analysis which is used for short term planning.

13.6.1 Marginal costing assumptions

When using marginal costing some general assumptions are made. Although these may be relaxed in particular circumstances, the following are normally applied:

1. Costs can be defined either as *fixed* or *variable* and they behave in a *consistent* fashion.
2. There is a *linear relationship* between costs and revenue, at least over the range of activity being considered.
3. No changes in the *efficiency* of production methods are introduced.
4. There are no changes in *stock levels*, or stock is valued at marginal cost.

Exercises

1. Define variable costs and fixed costs, giving four examples of each.
2. A company has the following semi-variable costs at two different levels of activity:

Production levels	Semi-variable costs
Units	£
2,500	20,000
5,000	25,000

   What are the variable cost and the fixed cost elements if 6,000 units are produced?
3. What are the main management decisions which can be helped by the use of marginal costing?
4. Seth plc manufactures a product with a selling price of £5.00 per unit. The variable costs are £2.00 for direct materials, £1.00 for direct labour and £1.00 for variable overheads. The fixed costs are £100,000 per annum. Prepare a marginal costing statement for a financial period when 120,000 units were produced.
5. The variable cost of the power drill manufactured by Hometools Ltd is £4 and the selling price £10. The company expects its net profit for the year just ending to be £275,000 after charging fixed costs amounting to £85,000.

The company's production capacity is not fully utilised and market research suggests three alternative strategies for the forthcoming year:

Strategy	Reduced selling price	Sales volume expected to increase by
1	5%	10%
2	7%	20%
3	10%	25%

(a) Assuming the same cost structure as the current year, evaluate the alternative strategies available to the company and state which is the most profitable.
(b) Suggest other considerations which management would probably have in mind when making its decision.

(ACCA, June 1978)

6. (a) Explain what you understand by the term 'cost behaviour', why it is important in the context of cost and management accounting, and what behaviour patterns may be encountered.
(b) What factors influence the behaviour of costs in response to changes in an organisation's level of activity?

(ACCA, June 1987)

7. A manufacturing company with a single product has the following sales and production results over three financial periods:

	Period 1 000 units	Period 2 000 units	Period 3 000 units
Sales	50	60	40
Production	70	40	60

The selling price per unit has remained at £10, and direct material and direct labour costs per unit at £5. All manufacturing overheads are absorbed into product cost at predetermined rates per unit of output. Any under/over absorbed balances are transferred to profit and loss in the period in which they arise. Variable manufacturing overhead absorption was predetermined at a rate of £1 per unit in each period. Fixed manufacturing overheads were expected to be £180,000 per period. Normal capacity is 60,000 units of output per period.

Manufacturing overheads actually incurred were as follows:

	Period 1 £000	Period 2 £000	Period 3 £000
Variable	68	45	60
Fixed	180	180	180

Assume that no further overheads are incurred (i.e., other than manufacturing overheads).

Required:
(a) Calculate the expected break-even point per period.
(b) Calculate the profit/loss that arose in each of the three periods.
(c) Reconcile your answers to (a) and (b) above, clearly demonstrating, explaining fully the reasons for, and commenting briefly upon, any differences encountered.

(ACCA, December 1985)

14 Marginal Costing and Decision Making

14.1 Contribution and Limiting Factors

The concept of 'contribution' is useful for decision making purposes, although there are occasions when it is necessary to modify the concept. This is because an organisation does not have unlimited growth potential: there are nearly always *constraints*.

The main limitation on a company's growth is often the *sales* it can achieve; the market will accept only a certain quantity of the product. But a company can also be limited in its activities by the scarcity of some *economic factor of production*; this could be a shortage of direct labour, materials or limited plant capacity.

When a factor constrains the growth of the company, this factor is known as the *key factor* (or **limiting factor**, or principal budget factor). Management must identify the limiting factor at any one time and arrange production so that the contribution per unit of limiting factor is maximised, as illustrated in Example 14.1.

Example 14.1

LDC Ltd has found an extremely rare mineral. The total world supply is only 20,000 tonnes. The company has a choice of using the mineral in the manufacture of either of two products, the details of which are:

	Product A £	Product B £
Selling price per unit	6.00	4.00
Variable costs per unit	2.00	2.50
Contribution per unit	4.00	1.50
Tonnes of material required	4	1

As product A gives a greater contribution per unit it would appear to be the better choice. But a limiting factor of materials is in operation (in this instance, a tonne can be used as a unit of the limiting factor). Product A gives a contribution of only £1.00 per tonne of material, whereas Product B gives a contribution of only £1.50 per tonne. If the rule is applied to maximise the contribution per unit of limiting factor Product B will be the better choice. By doing so, the total contribution from 20,000 tonnes of material available will be £30,000, against the possible total contribution from A of £20,000.

14.2 **Ranking of Products**

A company may have the choice of manufacturing *alternate products*. There are a number of different ways the products can be *ranked* to determine which would be the *most profitable* for the company to manufacture; the method to be used depends on the circumstances. The data in Example 14.2 is used to explain the four different ways of ranking used in practice in the modern business.

Example 14.2

A company has a choice of manufacturing one of two products. Based on the following information, which is preferable?

	Product A £	Product B £
Selling price per unit	15	30
Variable costs per unit:		
Materials	5	12
Labour	4	7
Overheads	1	3
Total cost	10	22
Contribution per unit	5	8

14.2.1 Ranking by contribution per unit

If there is no limitation on the sales of either of the units and no key factor operating on the resources used, the *absolute size of the unit contribution* can be used, and Product B in Example 14.2 would be selected.

14.2.2 Ranking by profit/volume ratio

If there is a maximum sales income which can be achieved from either product, the *profit/volume ratio* should be used to rank them. In

Example 14.2, if sales of £50,000 could be achieved of either Product A or Product B, the calculation would be:

$$\text{Profit/volume ratio} = \frac{\text{Contribution} \times 100}{\text{Sales}}$$

Product A $\dfrac{£5}{£15} = 33.\frac{1}{3}\%$ Product B $\dfrac{£8}{£30} = 26.7\%$

With sales of £50,000 the contribution from Product A is £16,650, but from Product B £13,350. In this instance, the company should choose Product A.

14.2.3 Ranking by total contribution

If the sales in units for each product are unequally limited, ranking should be by the *total contribution*. In Example 14.2, if sales of either 10,000 units of Product A or 6,000 units of product B could be achieved, Product A should be selected as this gives a total contribution of £50,000 compared to £48,000 from Product B.

14.2.4 Ranking by limiting factor

If a *limiting factor* is in operation it must be taken into consideration in the calculations. In Example 14.2, assuming that the same material is used for both products, differing only in the quantity used, the *contribution per unit of limiting factor* should be calculated:

	Product A £	Product B £
Contribution per unit	5.00	8.00
Material cost per unit	5.00	12.00
Contribution per £1 of materials	1.00	0.66

Product A should be selected as it gives a higher contribution per unit of limiting factor.

14.3 **Closure of an Activity**

A typical examination question provides the student with information on a company and asks whether, on the basis of the data provided, the student considers one of the company's activities should be ceased. The solution to this problem is to lay out the information in the form of a Marginal Cost Statement, as in Example 14.3.

Example 14.3

Neb Jake plc operates from one factory and manufactures three products. The profit and loss account for the year ended 31 December shows that product No. 3 has made a loss. The Managing Director suggests that the product should be dropped from their range. This would not affect the sales of the other products.

Profit and loss account
Year ended 31 December

	Product No. 1 £	Product No. 2 £	Product No. 3 £
Sales	100,000	70,000	130,000
Direct materials	32,000	16,000	54,000
Direct labour	22,000	20,000	58,000
Variable overheads	10,000	8,000	6,000
Fixed overheads	25,000	16,000	30,000
Total costs	89,000	60,000	148,000
Profit/(Loss)	11,000	10,000	(18,000)

The solution to this question is to assume that, in the absence of information to the contrary, fixed costs will remain the same in total for the company, even if one of the products is dropped. What must be calculated is the contribution, if any, each product makes to those *total fixed costs*. The figures therefore need to be redrafted to show this information.

Marginal cost statement
Year ended 31 December

	Product No. 1 £	Product No. 2 £	Product No. 3 £	Total £
Sales	100,000	70,000	130,000	300,000
Direct materials	32,000	16,000	54,000	102,000
Direct labour	22,000	20,000	58,000	100,000
Variable overheads	10,000	8,000	6,000	24,000
Total variable costs	64,000	44,000	118,000	226,000
Contribution	36,000	26,000	12,000	74,000
Less total fixed costs				71,000
Profit				3,000

It can be seen from this statement that Product No. 3 makes a contribution of £12,000 to fixed costs. If Product No. 3 was dropped, that contribution would be lost and the company would make a total loss of £9,000. The general rule is that if an activity makes a contribution towards fixed costs, it is worthwhile continuing. However, there are exceptions to this general rule which are examined in Chapter 15.

14.4 **Acceptance of a Special Order**

A company manufactures a product with variable costs of £8.00 per unit and a selling price of £10.50. A customer asks if they can have 2,000 units in addition to their ordinary order, but at a special price of £10.00 per unit. Should the company agree?

This problem raises complex issues on relationships with customers and the likely reaction of competitors, but from the financial point of view the solution is simple. As the variable costs of the product are £8.00, any selling price above this amount will give a contribution. The general rule is that if an activity gives a contribution it is worthwhile undertaking. On financial grounds, it is worthwhile accepting the order at the reduced selling price.

It would not make financial sense to agree to sell the product at a price less than the variable costs. To do so would mean a *negative contribution*. Similarly, if the company could supply the additional 2,000 units at

£10.00 only by reducing its present sales at £10.50 it would be reducing its total contribution by accepting the order and therefore should not do so.

14.5 Making or Buying a Product

Sometimes a company has the option of making a product or buying it direct from another company. This often occurs when the item is a component which is assembled as part of another product. Marginal costing can be used to assist the decision.

A company can make component X with variable costs of £9.00 per unit or it can purchase it from another manufacturer at £10.00 per unit. What should it do? If the company has idle capacity, it should make the product itself as the variable cost of £9.00 is lower than the buying price of £10.00. Fixed costs are excluded from the comparison as it is assumed that they will continue even when factory facilities are idle. The only additional costs incurred by the company in making the component will be the £9.00 variable costs per unit.

The rule that it is more profitable to manufacture if the variable costs are lower than the buying price holds true *only* if there is *idle capacity*. If the part can be made internally only by dropping production of another product, further analysis is required, as in example 14.4.

Example 14.4

Bruton plc can make component Z in 6 hours with variable costs of £10.00. The supplier's price for the component is £20.00. If Bruton decides to make the component it can do so only by sacrificing production of its main product 'Keto'. This product takes 25 hours to make and has variable costs of £150.00 and a selling price of £200.00. What is the correct financial decision for the company? On the face of it, the company should make Z as the variable costs are lower than the buy in price. But if it makes Z the company will lose the contribution from Keto which is £50.00 for 25 hours or £2.00 per hour. The calculation is:

	£
Cost of making Z	
Variable costs of component	10.00
Lost contribution (6 hours @ £2.00)	12.00
	22.00

As the supplier's price is only £20.00, it will be financially more worthwhile for Bruton to buy the component rather than make it.

This decision has been arrived at by bringing the lost contribution from Keto into the calculation. This is using the concept of **opportunity cost**, which represents the *value of the benefit given up* in favour of an alternative course of action.

Exercises

1. Describe the four different ways of ranking products, and the circumstances in which each one should be used.
2. What is meant by 'opportunity cost'?
3. A company, with no idle capacity, can manufacture a component with variable costs of £5.00 per unit. To purchase the unit from an outside supplier the price would be £6.80 per unit. To manufacture the component would mean that production of the main product would be reduced. The main product has a variable cost of £80.00 per unit and a selling price of £100.00 per unit. Ten components can be made in the time that it takes to make one unit of the main product. Should the company make or buy?
4. Mathews plc anticipates that it will produce 5,000 units per annum at a selling price of £6.00 each. At that level of production, the costs will be:

	£
Direct materials	1.60
Direct labour	2.00
Factory overheads: variable	0.80
fixed	0.30
Fixed administration and	
selling overheads	0.50
Total cost	5.20

   (a) A customer has placed a special order and has requested a discount price of £5.00 per unit. Should this order be accepted?
   (b) By reducing the selling price to £5.50 per unit, sales could be increased to 7,000 units without incurring additional fixed costs. Is this price reduction advisable?
5. Industrial Fitments Ltd produce three types of shelving – 'Factory', 'Stores' and 'Office', which are made from the same basic material, mild steel, which costs £1 per square metre. The standard unit cost of the three products are as follows:

	'Factory'	'Stores'	'Office'
	p	p	p
Direct material:			
Mild Steel	84	78	75
Attachments	14	25	30
Direct labour:			
Machining	10	15	19
Spraying	4	7	6
Unit selling prices are:	175	186	190

Sales expectations for the forthcoming month are:

	Units
'Factory'	2,000
'Stores'	2,400
'Office'	1,600

Owing to an industrial dispute, suppliers of mild steel have intimated that they will be able to supply only 2,500 square metres during the month.

You are required to:
(a) prepare a statement which will enable you to advise management on the most profitable production pattern to pursue;
(b) mention briefly the matters which should receive the attention of management when confronted with the type of situation described above.

(ACCA, June 1976)

6. *Exewye*
The summarised profit and loss statement for Exewye plc for the last year is as follows:

	£000	£000
Sales (50,000 units)		1,000
Direct materials	350	
Direct wages	200	
Fixed production overhead	200	
Variable production overhead	50	
Administration overhead	180	
Selling and distribution overhead	120	
	——	
		1,100
Loss for the year		(100)

At a recent board meeting, the directors discussed the year's results, following which the chairman asked for suggestions to improve the situation.

You are required, as management accountant, to evaluate the following alternative proposals and to comment briefly on each:

(a) Pay salesmen a commission of 10% of sales and thus increase sales to achieve break-even point.
(b) Reduce selling price by 10% which it is estimated would increase sales volume by 30%.
(c) Increase direct wage rates from £4 to £5 per hour, as part of a productivity/pay deal. It is hoped that this would increase production and sales by 20%, but advertising costs would increase by £50,000.
(d) Increase sales by additional advertising of £300,000, with an increased selling price of 20%, setting a profit margin of 10%.

(CIMA, May 1985)

7. The management of an engineering company manufacturing a range of products is considering next year's production, purchase and sales budgets. Shown below are the budgeted total unit costs for two of the components and two of the products manufactured by the company.

	Component 12 £ per unit	Component 14 £ per unit	Product VW £ per unit	Product XY £ per unit
Direct material	18	26	12	28
Direct labour	16	4	12	24
Variable overhead	8	2	6	12
Fixed overhead	20	5	15	30
	£62	£37	£45	£94

Components 12 and 14 are incorporated into other products manufactured and sold by the company, but not the two products shown above. it is possible to purchase Components 12 and 14 from another company for £60 per unit and £30 per unit respectively.

The anticipated selling prices of Products VW and XY are £33 and £85 respectively.

Required:
(a) Advise the management of the company whether it would be profitable to: (i) purchase either of the above components, (ii) sell either of the above products.
(b) State clearly, and where appropriate comment upon, the assumptions you have made in answering (a) above.
(c) Consider how the following additional information would affect your advice in (a) above:
  (i) Next year's budgeted production requirements for the two components are 7,000 units of Component 12 and 6,000 units of Component 14. Next year's budgeted sales for the two products are Product VW 5,000 units and Product XY 4,000 units.
  (ii) A special machine is used exclusively by the above two components and two products and for technical reasons the machine can only be allowed to operate for 80,000 machine hours next year. The budgeted usage of the machine is:

  Component 12 – 8 machine hours   Product VW – 6 machine hours
  Component 14 – 2 machine hours   Product XY – 12 machine hours

The operating costs of the machine have been included in the unit costs shown in (a) above.

(ACCA, June 1985)

8. A company is preparing its production budget for the year ahead. Two of its processes are concerned with the manufacture of three components which are used in several of the company's products. Capacity (machine hours) in each of these two processes is limited to 2,000 hours.

Production costs are as follows:

	Component		
	X	Y	Z
	£/unit	£/unit	£/unit
Direct materials	15.00	18.50	4.50
Direct labour	12.00	12.50	8.00
Variable overhead	6.00	6.25	4.00
Fixed overhead:			
Process M	6.00	6.00	4.50
Process N	10.50	10.50	3.50
	49.50	53.75	24.50

Requirements for components X, Y and Z for the following year are:

Component X	300 units
Component Y	300 units
Component Z	450 units

Fixed overhead is absorbed on the basis of machine hours at the following rates:

Process M	£3.00 per hour
Process N	£3.50 per hour

Components X and Z could be obtained from an outside supplier at the following prices:

Component X	£44.00 per unit
Component Z	£23.00 per unit

Required:

(a) Demonstrate that insufficient capacity is available to produce the requirements for components X, Y and Z in the year ahead, and calculate the extent of the shortfall.

(b) Determine the requirements for bought-in components in order to satisfy the demand for components at minimum cost.

(c) Consider briefly any other factors which may be relevant to decisions regarding these components in the longer term.

(ACCA, June 1986)

9. Symbols Ltd manufactures three products, Alpha, Beta and Gamma, the standard costs of which are as follows:

	Alpha £	Beta £	Gamma £
Materials	21	14	21
Labour:			
Machinists*	6	9	3
Assemblers†	3	4	2

The company's fixed overheads for the forthcoming year commencing 1 January 1977 are expected to amount to £100,000.

The marketing director has estimated that demand for the forthcoming year will be:

Alpha	6,000 at selling price of £50
Beta	10,000 at selling price of £45
Gamma	8,000 at selling price of £40

but the production director has pointed out that machine capacity is currently 88,000 hours per annum, although this will increase to 120,000 hours per annum when the new plan, already on order, is delivered, but this will not be during the year for which the budget is being prepared. However, the production director, anticipating the problem, has located a general engineering firm who are equipped to undertake work of appropriate quality and have quoted the following prices for production of the company's products on a sub-contracting basis:

Alpha	£40
Beta	£36
Gamma	£32

You are required to:

(a) advise the managing director how the services of the sub-contractor should be used to enable Symbols Ltd to meet the expected demand for its products in the most profitable manner, showing full details of the calculations upon which your advice is based;

(b) prepare a statement showing the profit to be expected if your advice is followed; and

(c) briefly explain the reasoning you have applied in making your recommendation.

* Machinists are paid £1.50 per hour.
† Assemblers are paid £1.00 per hour.

(*ACCA, December 1976*)

15 Break-even Analysis

15.1 Introduction

Break-even analysis is concerned with predicting costs, volume and profit *as the level of activity changes*. The theory of break-even analysis is derived from the principles of marginal costing, and the assumptions and definitions of fixed and variable costs and their behaviours discussed in earlier chapters are used.

Break-even analysis can be conducted by constructing a chart or applying a formula. A break-even chart shows the approximate profit or loss at different levels of activity. A formula is frequently used to calculate the **break-even point**; that is the level of activity at which the company makes neither profit nor loss, but *breaks even*.

Because break-even analysis uses assumptions of cost behaviour, there are limitations in its application. One of the most important limitations is that fixed and variable costs change their behaviour over a certain range of activity. For example, if production is doubled more factory space will be required with an increase in the associated fixed costs. Variable costs may also be affected if, for example, the company enters into bulk buying of materials at a discount.

The identification of the break-even point is not the sole purpose of break-even analysis. The behaviour of costs and profits at various levels of activity is of great importance to management and this information can be provided through the use of break-even analysis. However, the term *cost–volume–profit (C–V–P)* analysis is often preferred because it emphasises the *changes in relationships at different levels of activity*. In this chapter the term 'break-even analysis' is used, but students should be aware of the alternative.

15.2 Constructing a Break-even Chart

All costs must be divided into their fixed and variable elements, and some appropriate *measure of activity* must be selected. If possible, the unit of output should be used, although percentages of total capacity or other measures may have to be adopted. With information on fixed and variable costs, selling price and volumes, a break-even chart can be constructed, as in Example 15.1.

Example 15.1

A company manufactures a single product with a maximum production capacity of 2,000 units. The variable costs incurred are £5.00 per unit; the product sells at £10.00 each. During the financial period the fixed costs are £5,000.

The first stage is to draw on graph paper the horizontal axis marked with the levels of activity and the vertical axis with values in £s' for costs and revenues. The first line can then be drawn, which is the *fixed cost line*. Fixed costs are the same whatever the level of activity, so the line will be parallel to the horizontal axis. In this example, the fixed costs are £5,000 at nil output and the same figure at 2,000 units (Figure 15.1).

Fig 15.1   *Break-even chart – plotting fixed costs*

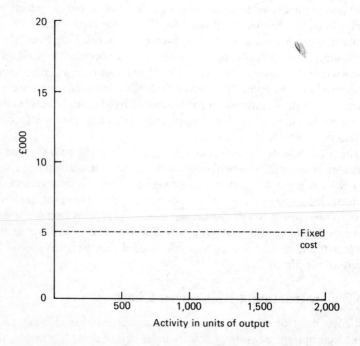

Variable costs must now be added to the fixed costs to give a *total cost line*. By drawing up a simple table, the total costs for different activity levels can be calculated and plotted on the graph.

Units	Fixed costs £	Variable costs £	Total costs £
0	5,000	0	5,000
500	5,000	2,500	7,500
1,000	5,000	5,000	10,000
1,500	5,000	7,500	12,500
2,000	5,000	10,000	15,000

Note that at nil activity the total costs are equal to the fixed costs as no variable costs have been incurred. When plotting the total costs on the graph only *two* points need be plotted, those at nil activity and at maximum activity, as the total cost line is a straight line (see Figure 15.2). At this stage, however, students may prefer to plot all the points calculated to minimise the possibility of error.

Fig 15.2 *Break-even chart – plotting the total cost line*

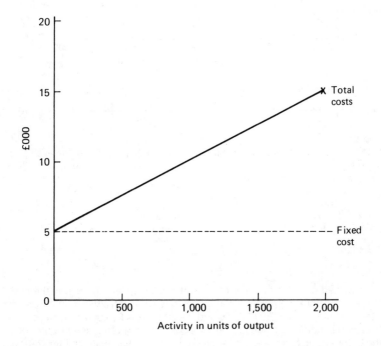

The final stage is to plot the *revenue line*. At nil activity there is no revenue. At 2,000 units activity is 2,000 × £10.00 per unit = £20,000. The point at which the total cost line and revenue line intersect is the *break-even point* – i.e., the level of activity where neither profit nor loss is made; in this instance 1,000 units (see Figure 15.3).

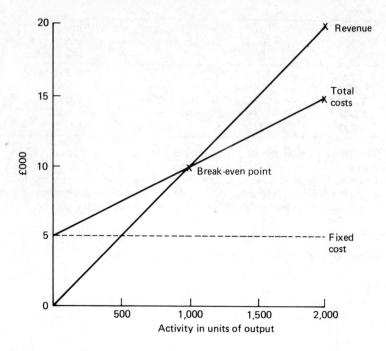

Fig 15.3   *Break-even chart – plotting the revenue line*

At this stage a small calculation can be made to prove that the break-even point is 1,000 units.

Calculation of the break-even point:

	£	£
Revenue (1,000 units @ £10.00)		10,000
Fixed costs	5,000	
Variable costs (1,000 @ £5.00)	5,000	10,000
Profit/(Loss)		

If we wished to know what the profit is at a selected level of activity the figure can be read from the graph. If the selected level of activity is 1,500 units, the total costs at this level are £12,500 and the revenue is £15,000. The profit figure of £2,500 is obtained by deducting total costs from revenue (see Figure 15.4). The difference in activity levels between the break-even point and the selected level of activity is known as the *margin of safety*. In this example, the margin of safety is 500 units – in other words, the company can drop 500 units from the selected level of activity before it starts to enter a loss.

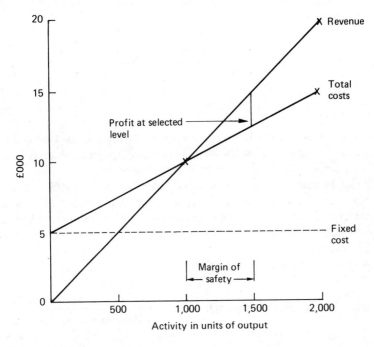

Fig 15.4   *Break-even chart – reading off the profit*

15.3 **Using Formulae**

Students will have realised from Example 15.1 that the construction of a break-even chart can lead to some inaccuracies in the answers because of the lack of precision in drawing the chart. Instead of drawing a chart, formulae can be used to calculate the answers. The formulae in this section are for a firm with a single product or an unvarying mix of sales and they are applied to the data given in section 15.2.

The break-even point can be expressed either in terms of units or sales value. To find the break-even point in units, the first stage is to calculate the *contribution per unit*:

	£
Selling price per unit	10.00
Variable costs per unit	5.00
Contribution per unit	5.00

The formula is:

$$\text{Break-even point} = \frac{\text{Fixed costs}}{\text{Contribution per unit}} = \frac{£5,000}{£5.00}$$

$$= 1,000 \text{ units}$$

This is the same answer as arrived at by constructing a break-even chart, but it can be appreciated that with more complex figures a greater degree of accuracy will be achieved by using calculations.

It may be that we want to know what the level of sales must be in order to break even. One way to do this is to multiply the number of units at break-even point by the selling price per unit. With 1,000 units selling at £10.00 each a total sales value of £10,000 would thus have to be achieved to break even.

Another method is to use the formula:

$$\text{Sales value at break-even point} = \frac{\text{Total fixed cost} \times \text{Sales value}}{\text{Total contribution}}$$

The amounts for sales value and contribution can be at the maximum level of activity, or per unit, or any other level. The formula is based on the Profit/Volume ratio discussed in Chapter 13, and gives:

$$\frac{£5,000 \times £10.00}{£5.00} = £10,000$$

Once the formulae for calculating the break-even point are understood, it is simple to calculate any other level of activity. In the examples above we have been attempting to find the level of activity which will allow recovery of the *fixed costs*. If we wish to recover more than the fixed costs – i.e., to have some *profit*, the formula is:

$$\text{Selected level of activity} = \frac{\text{Fixed costs} + \text{Target profit}}{\text{Contribution per unit}}$$

If we wish to make a profit of £2,500, the level of activity will be:

$$\frac{£5,000 \times £2,500}{£5.00} = 1,500 \text{ units}$$

Or in terms of sales value

$$\frac{£7,500 \times £10.00}{£5.00} = £15,000$$

15.4 Limitations of Break-even Analysis

Although break-even analysis can be a useful tool, there are a number of limitations which affect its value. These constraints can be grouped under three broad headings.

15.4.1 Measuring activity

If the company is manufacturing a *single, identifiable product*, the measure of activity is simply the unit of output. Frequently this situation does not exist, and alternative measures must be found. If there are a number of products, *direct labour hours* may be used as a measure of activity, although this raises problems of plotting the revenue line. If the sales mix is constant, activity may be usefully measured in £ of *sales*.

15.4.2 Managerial decisions

Although costs may be identified as fixed or variable, management can take decisions which will affect this division. Labour is often regarded as a variable cost, but in times of temporary shortages of work management may determine to retain labour at their normal pay rates so that the workforce is available when business picks up. Such a policy makes labour a *fixed cost*.

Another example of the impact of managerial decision making is the change to subcontract services. If a company provides its own service internally – for example, computer services – there will be a high element of *fixed cost*. If management decides to scrap its own service and hire outside services – for example, a computer bureau – it becomes primarily a *variable cost*.

15.4.3 The relevant range

The assumptions made about cost behaviour hold true only within a certain limited range of activity, known as the *relevant range*; variable costs may not give a straight line outside this range. Labour may be working overtime at enhanced pay rates, for example, thus causing variable costs to develop a curve. Direct materials may be purchased at a discount once the company exceeds a certain order limit.

Fixed costs may change at different levels of activity. Over the entire range of activity a company can achieve some of the fixed costs are likely to increase in steps. For example, an increase in production may require larger stores facilities and greater maintenance provision, with higher fixed costs.

Figure 15.5 shows how costs may behave over the complete range of activity and decisions should be made concerning those levels of activity only within the relevant range. Within this range, it is assumed that costs will behave in the predicted fashion.

15.5 **Alternative Break-even Charts**

The break-even charts constructed so far in this chapter are often referred to as 'traditional' break-even charts; the fixed line is plotted first, and the variable costs are added to this to plot the total cost line.

Fig 15.5   *Possible fixed cost behaviour*

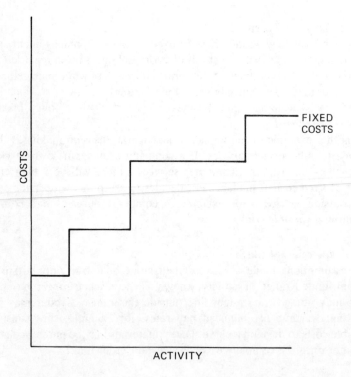

There are alternatives to this chart which use the same underlying principles and data, but present the information in a different way.

15.5.1 Contribution break-even chart
The contribution break-even chart is designed so that the *contribution figure at various levels of activity* can be read easily. The variable costs are plotted first, and the fixed costs added to them to give the total cost line. The difference between the variable cost line and the income line represents the *contribution wedge*. In Figure 15.6, the same figures are used as in the previous examples in this chapter.

15.5.2 The profit chart
Profit may be the most significant figure for management, but in the two variations of the break-even chart examined so far, profit can be calculated only by reading the income and total costs figures and making a deduction. The profit chart concentrates upon profit and the fixed, variable and total cost lines are not shown. The horizontal axis shows the

Fig 15.6   *Contribution break-even chart*

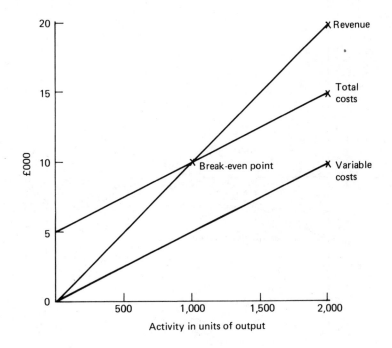

levels of activity, but the vertical axis shows profits and losses. The profit line is drawn from zero activity, where losses must be equal to fixed costs, and through the break-even point (see Figure 15.7).

Exercises

1. What is the margin of safety?
2. What is the relevant range?

Fig 15.7   *Profit chart*

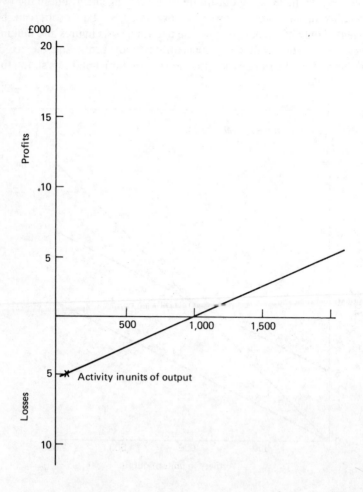

3. A company makes a product with a selling price of £5.00 per unit and variable costs of £3.00 per unit. The fixed costs for the period are £10,000. What must be the sales value for the company to make a profit of £2,000?

4. A company has fixed costs of £50,000 and produces one product with a selling price of £12.00 each and variable costs of £7.00 per unit. The maximum factory capacity is 20,000 units and it anticipates selling 15,000 units. Construct a break-even chart showing the break-even point and the margin of safety.

5. Criticially examine the assumptions underlying traditional break-even analysis, and consider the extent to which such analyses may be used effectively.

(ACCA, December 1979)

6. *Emcee*
Emcee plc manufactures three products, standard data for which are given below:

| | Per unit | | |
| | A | B | C |
	£	£	£
Direct materials	70	124	70
Direct wages:			
Department 1 at £3 per hour	15	24	18
Department 2 at £4 per hour	20	12	16
Variable overhead:		16	
Department 1 at £2 an hour	10	4	12
Department 2 at £1 per hour	5	30	4
Fixed overhead	35		20
	155	210	140
Profit	45	30	40
	200	240	180
Budgeted sales for the period (units)	1,200	800	900

You are required to:
(a) present one graph that shows the profit of the company as a whole and the contribution earned by each of the three products;
(b) advise management which product should be produced and state the total contribution for the period, if total hours in department 2 are limited to 12,000 and there are no such limitations in department 1.

(CIMA, May 1986)

7. *Local authority*
(a) Identify and discuss briefly five assumptions underlying cost-volume-profit analysis.
(b) A local authority, whose area includes a holiday resort situated on the east coast, operates, for 30 weeks each year, a holiday home which is let to visiting parties of children in care from other authorities. The children are accompanied by their own house mothers who supervise them throughout the holiday. From six to fifteen guests are accepted on terms of

£100 per person per week. No differential charges exist for adults and children.

Weekly costs incurred by the host authority are:

	£ per guest
Food	25
Electricity for heating and cooking	3
Domestic (laundry, cleaning, etc.) expenses	5
Use of minibus	10

Seasonal staff supervise and carry out the necessary duties at the home at a cost of £11,000 for the 30-week period. This provides staffing sufficient for six to ten guests per week but if eleven or more guests are to be accommodated, additional staff at a total cost of £200 per week are engaged for the whole of the 30-week period.

Rent, including rates for the property, is £4,000 per annum and the garden of the home is maintained by the council's recreation department which charges a nominal fee of £1,000 per annum.

You are required to:
 (i) tabulate the appropriate figures in such a way as to show the break-even point point(s) and to comment on your figures;
 (ii) draw, on graph paper, a chart to illustrate your answer to (b) (i) above.

(CIMA, May 1987)

8. A company produces and sells two products with the following costs:

	Product X	Product Y
Variable costs (per £ of sales)	£0.45	£0.60
Fixed costs	£1,212,000 per period	

Total sales revenue is currently generated by the two products in the following proportions:

Product X	70%
Product Y	30%

Required:
(a) Calculate the break-even sales revenue per period, based on the sales mix assumed above.
(b) Prepare a profit volume chart of the above situation for sales revenue up to £4,000,000. Show on the same chart the effect of a change in the sales mix to Product X 50%, Product Y 50%. Clearly lindicate on the chart the break-even point for each situation.

(c) Of the fixed costs £455,000 are attributable to Product X. Calculate the sales revenue required on Product X in order to recover the attributable fixed costs and provide a net contribution of £700,000 towards general fixed costs and profit.

(ACCA, June 1987)

16 Comparison of Marginal with Absorption Costing

16.1 Introduction

Absorption costing is a technique which charges *fixed costs* to *products or cost units*. The fixed overheads are either allocated or apportioned to cost centres. An *overhead absorption rate* is then used to charge the production cost centre costs to the cost units passing through them. Although the process is arbitrary, the result is that a cost unit is charged with what is deemed to be a fair share of the fixed overhead.

Marginal costing is concerned with the way that costs behave when there are changes in activity levels. Costs are divided into *variable* and *fixed* costs. Only variable costs are charged to the cost units and the contribution is calculated by deducting the variable costs from the revenue. Fixed costs are regarded as period costs unaffected by changes in levels of activity. The fixed costs are deducted from the total contribution for a period to arrive at the *profit* or *loss*.

Both absorption costing and marginal costing have their advantages and disadvantages and these are examined in this chapter. Both techniques can have a significant impact on the *valuation of stocks* and the *reporting of period profits*.

16.2 Main Features of Absorption and Marginal Costing

A comparison of the main features of the two techniques will permit a fuller discussion of their respective advantages and disadvantages.

16.2.1 Absorption costing

1. All costs are charged to the cost unit and a *profit* can be ascertained for *each unit*.
2. The *total profit* is equal to the sum of the profits from the individual cost units.
3. As output changes, so the *total cost per unit changes* because fixed costs are spread over the different number of units.
4. Work in progress and finished stocks valuation include a share of fixed costs and therefore are valued at *full production cost*.

16.2.2 Marginal costing

1. Only variable costs are charged to each cost unit and the contribution is ascertained for *each unit*.
2. The *total profit* is equal to the total contribution *minus* the fixed costs for the period.
3. As output changes the variable costs and contribution per unit are *constant*.
4. Work in progress and finished stocks valuations are at *variable production cost*; there is no inclusion of any fixed cost.

16.3 Arguments for Marginal Costing .

It should be noted that marginal costing is not necessarily 'better' than absorption costing, or vice versa. Although some practitioners will contend the superiority of one technique or the other, it is a matter of examining the circumstances in each case. The following list of arguments in favour of marginal costing must be balanced by the subsequent list in favour of absorption costing.

1. Fixed costs are a *period cost*, not a product cost, and should be written off in the period in which they occur.
2. Production has an impact only on *variable costs*, and therefore this is where the concentration should be.
3. Pricing decisions are improved because management can determine the *level at which a contribution is made*.
4. Changes in volume of activity do not affect the unit cost as only *variable costs* are involved and there is no spreading of fixed costs.
5. *Under or over absorption of overheads* does not arise. .
6. The *arbitrary apportionment of fixed costs* is avoided.

16.4 Arguments for Absorption Costing

1. Fixed costs represent a sacrifice to ensure that production can take place and therefore should be *included*.
2. Changes in production levels, particularly when they are significant, will have an *impact on fixed costs* and, decisions should take this into account.
3. In the long run, *fixed costs must be recovered* for the organisation to make a profit; concentration on recovering the variable cost per unit may obscure this fact.
4. Writing off fixed costs in the period in which they incur can lead to the reporting of losses, but the company may have been producing goods

for stock for sale later in the year – e.g., seasonal products for Christmas. A proportion of the fixed costs should be included in the *stock valuation* to give a more accurate representation.
5. Where capital expenditure is high, no knowledge of true product profitability can be ascertained unless *fixed costs* are included.
6. The *separation* of costs into their fixed and variable elements is not always possible.
7. *Statement of Standard Accounting Practice No. 9* recommends absorption costing for stock valuation for financial accounts.

16.5 Stock Valuations

If there is no stock or no changes in stock levels at the beginning and end of a period, marginal costing and absorption costing will give the same figure of profit for the period. If there are changes in the stock levels, the valuations of stock will differ and this will be reflected in the reported profit figure for the period (see Example 16.1).

Example 6.1

Fion plc manufactures a product 'Edita' which has a selling price of £6.00 each. For the month of January the figures are:

Total no. of units manufactured	10,000
Total no. of units sold	9,000
Production costs: variable	£25,000
fixed	£10,000
Fixed selling costs	£16,000

Marginal cost statement
for the month of January

	£	£
Sales		54,000
Variable costs of production	25,000	
Less closing stock	2,500	22,500
Contribution		31,500
Less fixed costs for period: Production	10,000	
Selling	16,000	26,000
Profit		5,500

Note that the value of the closing stock is calculated by multiplying the number of units (1,000) by the *variable cost per unit only* (£2.50). This is found by dividing the variable costs of production of £25,000 by the total number of units produced of 10,000.

*Absorption costing statement
for the month of January*

	£	£
Sales		54,000
Production costs: variable	25,000	
fixed	10,000	
	35,000	
Less closing stock	3,500	31,500
Gross profit		22,500
Fixed selling costs		16,000
Profit		6,500

Note that the value of the closing stock is calculated by multiplying the number of units by the *total cost of each unit*. The total cost consists of fixed and variable costs, so the total production cost of one unit is £35,000 divided by 10,000 units.

In absorption costing, a proportion of the fixed costs incurred in January in Example 16.1 are being transferred to the following period in the stock valuation. In marginal costing the total of the fixed costs are charged to production in the period in which they are incurred.

If at the end of a period there is an increase in the stock held by the company, the reported profit will be higher under absorption costing than under marginal costing, because of the treatment of fixed costs. Over a long period of time, total profits for the company will be the same under absorption costing and marginal costing because total costs will be the same. It is the profit for the *separate accounting periods* which will differ.

Exercises

1. What are the main features of marginal costing and absorption costing?
2. Explain the impact on profit of increases in stock at the end of a period under marginal costing compared to that under marginal costing.
3. What are the advantages of absorption costing?
4. The following data relates to a company for the month of January. Construct statements for the period using both marginal costing and absorption costing to show the figures of profit:

Sales	2,000 units
Production	2,500 units
Sales price	£5.00 per unit
Variable production costs	£3.00 per unit
Fixed production costs for the period	£2,500

5. Discuss the relative advantages of accounting systems based upon full absorption and marginal costing principles, and provide a simplified example for each system of the likely format of an income statement for management.

(ACCA, June 1986)

6. Shown below is next year's budget for the Forming and Finishing departments of Tooton Ltd. The departments manufacture three different types of component which are incorporated into the output of the firm's finished products.

Component	A	B	C
Production	14,000 units	10,000 units	6,000 units
Prime costs:	£ per unit	£ per unit	£ per unit
Direct materials			
— Forming Dept	8	7	9
Direct labour			
— Forming Dept	6	9	12
— Finishing Dept	10	15	8
	24	31	29

Manufacturing times:			
Machining			
— Forming Dept	4 hr per unit	3 hr per unit	2 hr per unit
Direct Labour			
— Forming Dept	2 hr per unit	3 hr per unit	4 hr per unit
— Finishing Dept	3 hr per unit	10 hr per unit	2 hr per unit

	Forming Department £	Finishing Department £
Variable overheads	200,900	115,500
Fixed overheads	401,800	231,000
	602,700	346,500

Machine time required and available	98,000 hr	—
Labour hours required and available	82,000 hr	154,000 hr

The Forming Department is mechanised and employs only one grade of labour, the Finishing Department employs several grades of labour with differing hourly rates of pay.

Required:

(a) Calculate suitable overhead absorption rates for the Forming and Finishing Departments for next year and include a brief explanation for your choice of rates.

(b) Another firm has offered to supply next year's budgeted quantities of the above components at the following prices:

Component A £30, Component B £65, Component C £60

Advise management whether it would be more economical to purchase any of the above components from the outside supplier. You must show your workings and, considering cost criteria only, clearly state any assumptions made or any aspects which may require further investigation.

(c) Critically consider the purpose of calculating production overhead absorption rates.

(ACCA, June 1980)

7. Mahler Products has two manufacturing departments each producing a single standardised product. The data for unit cost and selling price of these products are as follows:

		Department A	Department B
		£	£
Direct material cost		4	6
Direct labour cost		2	4
Variable manufacturing overheads		2	4
Fixed manufacturing overheads		12	16
Factory cost		20	30
Profit mark-up	50%	10	25% 7.50
Selling price		30	37.50

The factory cost figures are used in the departmental accounts for the valuation of finished goods stock.

The departmental profit and loss accounts have been prepared for the year to 30 June 1985. These are given below separately for the two halves of the year.

Mahler Products
Departmental profit and loss accounts Year to 30 June 1985

| | 1 July – 31 December 1984 | | 1 January – 30 June 1985 | |
| | Dept A | Dept B | Dept A | Dept B |
	£000	£000	£000	£000
Sales revenue	300	750	375	675
Manufacturing costs				
Direct material	52	114	30	132
Direct labour	26	76	15	88
Variable overheads	26	76	15	88
Fixed overheads	132	304	132	304
	236	570	192	612
Factory cost of production	60	210	120	180
Add	296			792
Opening stock of finished goods		780	312	
Less	120	180	20	300
Closing stock of finished goods	176	600	292	492
Factory cost of goods sold	30	100	30	100
Administrative and selling costs	206	700	322	592
Net profit	94	50	53	83

The total sales revenue was the same in each six monthly period but in the second half of the year the company increased the sales of Department A (which has the higher profit mark-up) and reduced the sales of Department B (which has the lower profit mark-up). An increase in company profits for the second six months was anticipated but the profit achieved was £8,000 lower for the second half of the year than for the first half. The profit for Department A fell by £41,000 while the profit for Department B rose by £33,000. There has been no change in prices of inputs or outputs.

You are required:
(a) to explain the situation described in the last paragraph – illustrate your answer with appropriate supporting calculations, and
(b) to redraft the departmental profit and loss accounts using marginal cost to value unsold stock.

(ACCA, December 1985)

17 Budgetary Control

17.1 Definitions

Managers are concerned for the *future success* of their company. They will assess the challenges and opportunities facing them and set *goals*, usually expressed in financial terms, that they intend to achieve. They will monitor the progress of the company towards these goals and take action to improve performance or revise goals if they have become unrealistic.

This process is known formally as **budgetary control**. This may be defined as the setting of plans (or *budgets*) which lay down policies for which managers are responsible. A continuous comparison is made of what is actually achieved with the plan, so that individual managers can remedy any divergence from the plan, or revise the plan if necessary.

The plan or budget is expressed in *monetary terms* and normally gives the income and/or the expenditure, including any capital expenditure, needed during a financial period to achieve the given objective. The period of time for which the budget is intended is known as the *budget period*, and the budget must be prepared and approved before this period of time begins.

Managers normally consider their plans and objectives over a long time of, say, five years. These long range plans are broken down into periods of one year and budgets drawn up in detail, normally subdivided into months, so that monitoring and control can be conducted.

Budgets are drawn up showing the income or expenditure for *individual functions* of the organisation – e.g., sales budget, production budget. As well as these functional budgets there are budgets for capital expenditure, stock holdings and cash flow. All the budgets are inter-related and incorporated into the *master budget*, which consists of the budgeted operating statements and balance sheet.

17.2 Objectives of Budgetary Control

Although the essence of budgetary control is in the planning and control of activities, the technique is so fundamental to good management practices that a number of objectives can be identified.

17.2.1 Planning
The setting of plans is a complex, time consuming and difficult activity. It is essential that management carries out this task, and a formal system of budgetary control ensures that they do so in a *systematic and logical fashion*.

17.2.2 Coordination
By setting plans, the activities of the various functions of the business can be *coordinated*. This means, for example, that production manufactures the right quantity of the required product for the sales team.

17.2.3 Communication
As individual managers are given the responsibility of achieving the plan, they must be informed of the *policies* of the organisation, the *constraints* under which it is operating and the *goals* that it intends to achieve. Without a method for communicating this information to managers, the system of budgetary control will fail.

17.2.4 Motivation
By setting clear targets and communicating them to employees, *motivation* may be improved. An organisation which has no sense of direction will find it difficult to motivate employees.

17.2.5 Identifying variances
When actual activity for a period of time is compared to the original plan, there will often be a difference expressed in financial terms. This difference is known as a **variance** and the examination of the variances will show whether management need to take any action.

17.2.6 Control
Rigorous control can be implemented only by setting a plan of what is intended to be achieved in a defined period of time and regularly *monitoring progress* against this plan with corrective action being taken when necessary.

17.3 Preparing Budgets

It is essential that budgetary control and the preparation of budgets is not regarded as the sole responsibility of the accounting function. The *whole management team* should be involved, with the accounting function normally providing a coordinating role and providing quantitative and financial data when needed.

A *Budget Committee* may be formed, comprising the functional heads of the company with the chief executive as the chairman. It is normal to appoint a Budget Controller who acts in a secretarial role and arranges for the provision of the information required for decision making. The Budget Controller is frequently an accountant, because knowledge of systems and procedures and access to data are required.

During preparation of the budgets it is important to identify any limiting factors and to ensure the best coordination of the various functions. The *limiting factor* or *principal budget factor* is that which prevents the company achieving higher levels of performance in the budget period; a shortage of materials, for example, or inadequate plant capacity may be the limiting factor, and decisions must be taken at an early stage to minimise the impact.

Once the principal budget factor has been identified and individual functional budgets are being set, it is important to ensure that *coordination of functions* takes place. It would not make sense, for example, to set a sales budget with a sales volume in excess of existing plant capacity, unless decisions were made on improving capacity, subcontracting work or cutting back on the sales budget.

The extent to which employees at various levels should be involved in the budget preparation is a matter of debate. Some commentators argue that fullest involvement of employees at the earliest stage makes for more realistic budgets and leads to greater motivation. With time constraints and the complexities of coordinating various plans, it is not normally practicable to involve all employees. This method of 'bottom up' budgeting, therefore usually starts with the functional heads setting plans for subsequent debate, amendment and coordination.

The alternative method to 'bottom up' planning is 'top down', where the board of the company sets specific targets and budgets are prepared to conform to these. In many companies a mix of 'bottom down' and 'top up' approaches is used, perhaps with functional heads identifying possible targets in broad terms at an early stage and the board considering these before detailed budgets are constructed.

17.4 Interrelationship of Budgets

The functional and other budgets adopted and approved by the board is incorporated into the *Master Budget*, which comprises the Budgeted Operating Statement for the period and the Budgeted Balance Sheet.

Although budgets for such activities as research and administration are not totally connected to the other budgets, they must be kept within limits directed by general policy and an interrelationship exists.

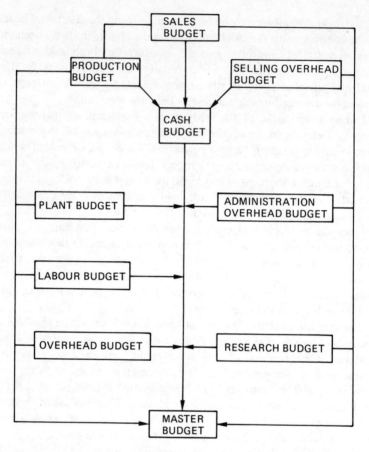

Fig 17.1   *Interrelationship of budgets*

In Figure 17.1 the level of sales have been taken as the limiting factor and the other budgets stem from this.

Notes

1. The *sales budget* is set first and shows what quantities can be sold and at what price.
2. The *production budget* is based on the sales budget, but policy changes on stock levels could lead to volume changes compared to the sales budget.

3. The production budget may reveal immediate plant shortages which have to be incorporated into a capital expenditure budget. A *capital expenditure budget* is required on a long-term basis in any event.
4. *General policies* dictate the limits of administration and research budgets, but they bear some relationship to the sales budget.
5. The individual budgets are assembled and incorporated into the *Master Budget*.

17.5 Advantages of Budgetary Control

It is possible to implement a system of budgetary control and for management to become disillusioned about the claimed benefits. Care, commercial sense and a knowledge of the particular company are required to ensure that budgetary control is properly implemented, so that it may provide the following advantages:

1. Decisions are based on an early study of the *future problems* and opportunities facing the company.
2. *Motivation* of the entire management team is assured, with clearly defined goals and a method of monitoring achievement.
3. Policies can be periodically examined in the light of changing circumstances, and *restated* if necessary.
4. The resources of the company are given the *fullest and most economical use*.
5. This control system embraces *every activity* of the company.
6. All the various functions within the organisation are *coordinated*.
7. Capital and effort are channelled into the most *profitable use*.

17.6 Disadvantages of Budgetary Control

Although budgetary control can offer many advantages, there are difficulties and pitfalls connected with its operation:

1. *Planning is not an exact science* and, although forecasting techniques such as time series analysis and exponential smoothing may assist, the problems should not be overlooked.
2. The process of *budgetary control* is time consuming and managers may believe that time could be better spent getting on with the job.
3. *Top management must be committed* to the system and to the budgets for the period, or there will be no sense of motivation or cooperation at other levels of management.
4. Budgets, once set, can appear *inflexible* and act as a constraint on management initiative.

5. *Variances* can arise through unrealistic plans and changed circumstances, and the reporting of such variances can demotivate managers.

Exercise

1. Shown below is an extract from next year's budget for a company manufacturing two products in two production departments.

Product	A	B
Sales	11,500 units	15,750 units
Opening stock	1,000 units	2,000 units
Closing stock (at end of budget year)	1,500 units	1,250 units

	£ per unit	£ per unit
Selling price	140	80
Prime costs:		
Materials	14	26
Labour – Production Department 1	20	8
– Production Department 2	18	12

Hourly wage rates for direct operatives are budgeted at £4 per hour in Production Department 1 and £3 per hour in Production Department 2. It should be assumed that all prime costs are variable.

Budgeted annual overheads:	Production Dept. 1	Production Dept. 2
	£	£
Fixed overheads	315,000	613,800
Variable overheads	67,500	145,200
	382,500	759,000

The company operates a full absorption costing system and each production department charges its budgeted overhead to products by means of a departmental direct labour hour absorption rate.

Production and overheads are budgeted to occur evenly throughout the year. However, monthly sales do vary and the budgeted sales for the first month are, Product A 1,200 units and Product B 2,300 units.

The total cost per unit of the opening stocks is Product A £98 per unit and Product B £75 per unit. These stock values are based upon the costs in the current period and are *not* the budgeted unit costs for the next year.

Required:
(a) Calculate the budgeted profit for the first month of next year for the above company. Any necessary assumptions should be clearly indicated.

(b) Calculate the effect on the above budgeted profit if in the first month, the actual results are as predicted except that actual production of Product B is 50 units higher than the budget.

(c) The accountant of the above company is considering changing from a full absorption costing system to a marginal costing system in which each month's fixed overheads will be written off immediately they are incurred. Describe the effect of the above proposal on the first month's budgeted profit and explain the reason for that effect. (Calculations are not required and candidates should assume that the opening stock values would be reduced to marginal cost *before* the first month's budgeted profit is calculated.)

(ACCA, June 1985)

18 Budgets

18.1 Introduction

Management may prepare budgets for the business as a whole and for particular aspects of it; there may be budgets for functions such as production, cash, capital expenditure, manpower and for other activities. Despite the apparent differences in the nature of the activities, the basic principles in setting and operating the budgets are the same.

Plans are set for the various activities. The initial plans may be in quantities – e.g., number of units to be sold – to be transferred into monetary terms subsequently. Most plans cover a period of one year, although activities such as capital expenditure and research may be for five years or longer.

These annual plans need to be subdivided into *shorter periods for monitoring and control*. It is usual to do this on a monthly basis and the spreading of the annual figures over 12 months is known as 'phasing the budget'. Normally it is insufficient to take the annual figure and divide by 12 to give the monthly figures. Most businesses experience peaks and troughs during the year, and this needs to be reflected in the monthly budget figures.

Actual progress is measured from the commencement of the budget period. This is compared with the plan for the month and the figures reported to the managers responsible. The differences between the actual and the budget figures are known as *variances*. If actual costs are below budget the variances are known as *favourable variances*: this is because the final profit figure should be *higher* than the budgeted profit.

When actual costs are above the budget figures the variances are *adverse*, and may be shown in parentheses (the figures are in brackets) in the management report. The adverse variances will cause the actual profit to be *lower* than the budgeted profit.

If the budget report shows income as well as costs, there may be variances for the income, but these will be the reverse of the costs variances. If actual income is above the budget figures, the variance is thus favourable because the actual profit will be higher than the budget.

Example 18.1 demonstrates the key points which can be identified in a budget report. This report is for one period only, but in many companies the monthly budget report gives the figures for the entire year divided into months, the actual figures to date and a cumulative column which shows the actual totals compared with the budget totals for the year to date.

Example 18.1

Budget report
January

Item	Budget £	Actual £	Variance £
Income – Product A	25,000	24,500	(500)
Income – Product B	18,000	17,200	(800)
Income – Product C	19,000	19,600	600
Total income	62,000	61,300	(700)
Costs – Salaries	28,400	29,000	(600)
– Expenses	12,500	12,000	500
– Admin.	1,800	1,700	100
– Misc.	700	300	400
Total costs	43,400	43,000	400
Profit	18,600	18,300	(300)

18.2 Cash budgets

Cash is the most essential resource of a business. Without sufficient cash a business will be *unable to operate*; an excess of cash means that there is inefficiency and a subsequent impairment of profitability. Even small companies without a budgetary control system will have some form of cash budget.

A cash budget shows the cash (including cheques) coming into the organisation and the cash going out. The cash coming in is termed **positive cash flow** and the cash going out is termed **negative cash flow**. The difference between these two flows is known as the **net cash flow**.

The exact form of the cash budget will vary from company to company, but the layout in Example 18.2 is typical. The cash budget is drawn up for the year and subdivided into monthly or even weekly amounts. For clarity Example 18.2 shows only the first three months.

Example 18.2

J. Christie starts a small retailing business with £5,000 she has in the bank. Her sales and purchases for the first three months are:

	Sales £	Purchases £
January	10,000	5,000
February	12,000	6,000
March	18,000	9,000

She has to pay for the purchases in the month in which they are made. Of her sales, 50% of the customers pay cash and the remainder pay in the month following the month of sale.

She rents a shop for £2,500 quarterly payable on the first day of the quarter. The running costs of the shop are £1,000 per month, payable in the month after month in which they occur. She pays wages of £500 per month payable in the month.

Cash budget January to March

Item	January £	February £	March £
Cash in			
Cash sales	5,000	6,000	9,000
Credit sales	—	5,000	6,000
Total cash in	5,000	11,000	15,000
Cash out			
Purchases	5,000	6,000	9,000
Rent	2,500	—	—
Running costs	—	1,000	1,000
Wages	500	500	500
Total cash out	8,000	7,500	10,500
Balance b/f	5,000	2,000	5,500
Net cash flow	(3,000)	3,500	4,500
Balance c/f	2,000	5,500	10,000

Note that the bottom three rows show how much Christie starts the month with (her £5,000 savings in January); the net cash flow for the month; and the balance at the end of the month which is carried forward as the opening balance for the following month.

The cash budget for Christie indicates that she will require at least £3,000 savings to start the business because of the negative cash flow in January. As she has £5,000 in the bank, the business appears viable. In February and March there are positive cash flows and Christie should be deciding before the budget period starts how the surplus cash flows should be used.

18.3 **Production Budgets**

When deciding upon the level of production there are two main considerations:

1. Whether the production levels in each subperiod will be *even* or *uneven*. Assuming an annual budget, most companies prefer to manufacture the same quantities each month to arrive at the annual figure. This even flow ensures that labour and machines are employed at optimum capacity. In seasonal industries, it may be necessary to have an uneven production flow, with peaks and troughs during the year.
2. The *amount of stock to be held*. This depends on a number of factors including the cash available, storage capacity, delivery times, possibility of shortages, etc.

18.3.1 Uneven production flows
If the level of sales is the limiting factor and a decision has been taken on the level of stock holding, with uneven production flows a simple calculation is required to determine the production levels for each period (see Example 18.3).

Example 18.3

Wheelers plc, a manufacturer of cycle panniers, has decided that the stock level should not fall below 500 units. At the beginning of January it has 600 units in stock and the budgeted sales for the month are 2,000 units. What should the production level for the month be?

	Units
Closing stock required at end of January	500
Add budgeted sales for the month	2,000
	2,500
Less opening stock at beginning of month	600
production requirement for the month	1,900

18.3.2 Even production flows
When a company wishes to produce the same quantity each month and has decided its minimum stock level, the problem is to determine the *opening quantity of stock* to ensure that sales needs are met (see Example 18.4).

Example 18.4

Chillproof plc manufactures window frames and has set a monthly production level of 50 units and does not want the stock level to fall below 100 units. The sales budget shows the following figures:

	Units
January	40
February	40
March	60
April	80
May	100
June	60

What should the opening stock in January be so that the company can meet its sales targets?

The way to tackle this problem is to set out the known information in the form of a *simple budget*:

	Jan.	Feb.	Mar.	Apr.	May	Jun.
Opening stock						
Production	50	· 50	50	50	50	50
Total						
Less Sales	40	40	60	80	100	60
Closing stock						

As the stock level must not fall below 100 units, we can start by inserting this figure as the opening stock in January and carry the calculations through to the end:

	Jan.	Feb.	Mar.	Apr.	May	Jun.
Opening stock	100	110	120	110	80	30
Production	50	50	50	50	50	50
Total	150	160	170	160	130	80
Less Sales	40	40	60	80	100	60
Closing stock	110	120	110	80	30	20

An opening stock of 100 units would be insufficient; this means that in three of the months stocks fall below the minimum level. June is the month with the lowest stock of only 20 units and a further 80 units are required to meet the stock holding of 100 units. The opening stock in January must therefore be 180 units.

18.4 Flexible Budgets

A budget may be fixed in that *once it has been established it is not changed*, even though there may be changes in activity levels; it may be revised if the situation so demands, but it is not changed solely because actual activity levels differ from the budget.

A **flexible budget** changes in accordance with *levels of activity*, and reflects the different behaviours of fixed and variable costs. A flexible budget may be used at the planning stage to illustrate the impact of achieving different activity levels. A flexible budget can also be used at the control stage at the end of a month to compare the actual results with what they should have been.

Flexible budgeting provides clearer information to management for decision making and control purposes. By comparing the actual results with what should have been achieved at that level of activity, a more accurate measure is given (see Example 18.5).

Example 18.5

Roberto's Pastas has set the following budget for the month of January based on sales of 90 units:

	£
Revenue	900
Variable costs	450
Variable overheads	90
Fixed overheads	300
Total costs	840
Profit	60

The actual sales for the month were 100 units, and the results are shown compared to the fixed budget:

	Fixed Budget £	Actual £
Revenue	900	1,000
Variable costs	450	530
Variable overheads	90	110
Fixed overheads	300	300
Total costs	840	940
Profit	60	60

The company may feel very pleased that it has achieved the budgeted profit, but a flexible budget can give a more accurate picture. It is constructed by changing the variable costs total and income to correspond with the *actual level of activity achieved*:

	Flexible budget £	Actual £
Revenue (£10 per unit)	1,000	1,000
Variable costs (£5 per unit)	500	530
Variable overheads (£1 per unit)	100	110
Fixed overheads	300	300
Total costs	900	940
Profit	100	60

The flexible budget shows that at the level of activity of 100 units the company should have achieved a profit of £100.

Exercises

1. What are the advantages of flexible budgets?
2. What matters do management need to consider when setting a production budget?
3. Juliet Miles has savings of £10,000 and she has decided to open a retailing business. The predicted sales and purchases for the first six months are:

	Sales £	Purchases £
January	15,000	8,000
February	15,000	8,000
March	15,000	10,000
April	20,000	10,000
May	20,000	12,000
June	20,000	12,000

She predicts that 10% of the sales will be for cash and the remaining 90% will be paid in the month following the month of sales. Purchases must be paid for in the month in which they occur. Rent of the shop will be £12,000 per annum payable quarterly in advance. Wages will be £500 payable each month. The electricity charge will be £1,000 payable at the end of each quarter. Telephone and postage charges will be £2,000 payable at the end of each quarter. Construct a cash budget.

4. Kerryblue Ltd is a company manufacturing two products using one type of material and one grade of labour. Shown below is an extract from the company's working papers for the next period's budget.

Product	K	B
Budgeted sales	3,000 units	4,500 units
Budgeted material consumption, per product	6 kilos	2 kilos
Budgeted material cost; £3 per kilo		
Standard hours allowed, per product	5 hours	3 hours

The budgeted wage rate for the direct workers is £4 per hour for a forty-hour week, overtime premium is 50% and there are 65 direct operatives.

The target productivity ratio (or efficiency ratio) for the productive hours worked by the direct operatives in actually manufacturing the products is 90%; in addition the amount of non-productive down-time is budgeted at 20% of the productive hours worked.

There are twelve 5-day weeks in the budget period and it is anticipated that sales and production will occur evenly throughout the whole period.

At the beginning of the period it is anticipated that the stocks will be:

Product K	1,050 units
Product B	1,200 units
Raw material	3,700 kilos

The target closing stocks, expressed in terms of the anticipated activity during the budget period are:

Product K	15 days sales
Product B	20 days sales
Raw material	10 days consumption

Required:
(a) Calculate the material purchase budget and the wages budget for the direct workers, showing both quantities and values, for the next period.
(b) Describe the additional information required in order to calculate the weekly cash disbursements for materials and wages during the above budget period.

(ACCA, June 1981)

5. *Clothar*
(a) Clothar plc manufactures one standard product and in common with other companies in the industry is suffering from the current depression in the market. Currently it is operating at a normal level of activity of 70% which represents an output of 6,300 units but the sales director believes that a realistic forecast for the next budget period would be a level of activity of 50%.

	Level of activity		
	60%	70%	80%
	£	£	£
Direct materials	37,800	44,100	50,400
Direct wages	16,200	18,900	21,600
Production overhead	37,600	41,200	44,800
Administration overhead	31,500	31,500	31,500
Selling and distribution overhead	42,300	44,100	45,900
Total cost	165,400	179,800	194,200

Profit is 20% of selling price.

You are required, from the data given in the current flexible budget above, to prepare a budget based on a level of activity of 50%, which should show clearly the contribution which could be expected.

(b) Discuss briefly three problems which may arise from such a change in level of activity.

(CIMA, May 1984)

6. (a) At the end of December the management accountant has in front of him the company's budgeted profit and loss account figures for each of the months from the following January to June. The July and August budgets follow the same pattern as that for June. The budgets can be summarised as follows:

	Jan.	Feb.	Mar.	Apr.	May	Jun.
Sales quantity	2,500	2,500	3,500	5,000	7,500	4,000
Production quantity	3,000	3,500	4,500	5,000	5,000	4,000
	£	£	£	£	£	£
Sales revenue	30,000	30,000	42,000	60,000	90,000	48,000
Factory Cost of production	28,500	33,250	42,750	47,500	47,500	38,000
Stock adjustment	(4,750)	(9,500)	(9,500)		23,750	
Factory Cost of goods sold	23,750	23,750	33,250	47,500	71,250	38,000
Selling and distribution costs	2,250	2,250	2,350	2,500	2,750	2,400
Admin. costs	3,000	3,000	3,000	3,000	3,000	3,000
Profit	1,000	1,000	3,400	7,000	13,000	4,600
	30,000	30,000	42,000	60,000	90,000	48,000

The budgeted factory fixed overhead for the year is £140,000 and this is absorbed into the factory cost of production at the rate of £3.50 per unit.

£32,000 of this overhead is depreciation of machinery and buildings, the remainder arises evenly throughout the year and is paid as it arises. Month end balances representing budgeted under or over absorbed overhead are carried forward and for the year as a whole the budgeted overhead is fully absorbed by the budgeted production. One quarter of the variable factory cost of production is direct material cost and the balance is predominantly manufacturing labour and similar services that are paid for as they arise. The planned direct material purchases of one month are determined by the planned production of the subsequent month. Suppliers are normally paid 30 days after the receipt of goods but it is possible to delay payment in some cases for another month. This course of action is resorted to only sparingly as the company does not wish to spoil its credit standing. 20% of the purchases attract a 5% discount for prompt (i.e., immediate) settlement. 75% of customers settle their accounts in the month following the sale, 20% take another month's credit and the remaining 5% pay in the third month following the sale.

The company normally pays an interim dividend at the end of June and it is anticipated that the net payment to be made in the forthcoming June will be £30,000.

You are required to prepare the company's Cash Budget for the months of April, May and June assuming that the cash balance at the start of April is estimated at £5,000 and the company's policy is to maintain a month end cash balance no lower than £4,000 and no higher than £10,000. Surplus cash can be invested on a short-term basis at 10%p.a. interest. No recognition has been given in the budgeted profit and loss accounts to any discount receivable or short term loan interest.

(b) Discuss and describe the possible use of a spread sheet computer package in the development of an organisation's cash budgets.

(*ACCA, June 1985*)

19 Standard Costing – Materials and Labour

19.1 Introduction

Standard costing is closely associated with budgetary control and few systems of standard costing would be in operation without a budgetary control system being present. Budgetary control, however, is used mainly by departments and businesses as a whole over a period of time and is a technique which can be used by itself in any organisation, including charities, universities, transport undertakings, etc.

Standard costing is mainly applied to products and processes and *predetermined costs and sales* are compared with actual costs and sales to establish the differences or *variances*. Managers within the company can be held responsible for these variances and, by analysing the reasons for the variances, control can be achieved.

The predetermined costs are known as *standard costs*, and these establish what costs should be in *specified working conditions*. The standard cost is calculated from technical specifications which give the quantity of materials, labour and other elements of cost required, and relate these to the prices and wage rates it is anticipated will be current for the period in which the standard cost is to be used.

The types of standards used by a company will depend upon its philosophy. Although a 'standard' is a measurable quantity established in defined conditions, a company may determine to set either *ideal standards* or *attainable standards*. Ideal standards are based upon the best possible working conditions, and no allowances are made for such difficulties as machine breakdowns and material wastage. Although useful for management decision making, ideal standards are not frequently used as employees may be demotivated by the impossibility of achieving them. Attainable standards are widely used in industry as they are based upon realistic efficient performance with allowances made for machine breakdown, etc.

19.2 Advantages of Standard Costing

1. A *benchmark* is established against which actual costs can be compared.

2. In setting standards a rigorous and searching examination of the company's *production activities* is carried out.
3. As the standards are based on future plans and expectations, the information provided to management is much more *accurate* than that based merely on past performance.
4. By examining the reasons for the differences (known as **variance analysis**) between standard costs and revenues and the actual figures, management need concentrate only on the *exceptions* to the planned performance, thus leading to greater managerial efficiency.
5. *Control over costs* is improved and reductions may be implemented by the use of variance analysis.

19.3 Disadvantages of Standard Costing

1. *Standards may be difficult to set*, particularly in a new or fast moving company.
2. The system may be very *costly* to maintain and the proliferation of *record keeping* may be regarded as an unwelcome burden by managers.
3. Standards can become *out of date* and require revision. In a particularly turbulent environment the standards may be outdated so quickly that managers have no confidence in the system.
4. Information provided by the system is of value only if it is *used* by managers for control purposes; if the information has no credibility or is not understood, it has no value.

19.4 Variance Analysis

Variance analysis is the investigation of the factors which have caused the *differences between standard and actual results*. It is important that variances are analysed into their constituent parts so that sufficient information is provided for a proper management investigation.

Favourable variances are those that have an impact which improves the predetermined profit. *Adverse* variances are those that have an impact of reducing the predetermined profit. The nature of the variance and its cause – e.g., material prices – must be reported quickly to the manager responsible so that the reason can be discovered – e.g., use of wrong quality of material – and effective action can be taken promptly. Both adverse and favourable variances should be investigated as they both represent a *deviation from the standard* which requires explanation.

The calculation of variances and a description of their purpose is fairly simple for most students. It is somewhat more difficult to interpret variances, as this requires practical experience. It is important when interpreting variances to remember that they are *interrelated*, and a variance in one aspect will often be reflected elsewhere. For example, if the *price paid for material is higher* than planned because the quality is better, it may be that a smaller quantity of this superior material is used, so there is *less wastage*.

19.5 **Direct Material Variances**

The basic concept behind the direct materials variances is the formula:

Total materials cost = Quantity used × Unit price

Standards are set both for the quantity of materials consumed for a specific volume of production, and for the price to be paid per unit of direct material.

When production for a period has been completed and the actual total material cost is compared to the standard material cost, there is likely to be a difference. This total cost variance may be because the *actual quantity* of material used is different from the standard, or because the *actual price* paid per unit is different from the standard, or a combination of the two factors.

The total variance can be broken down into a usage variance and a price variance (Figure 19.1).

Fig 19.1   *Material variance and price variance*

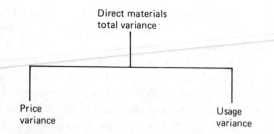

19.6 **Calculation of Direct Material Variances**

19.6.1 **Direct material price variance**
This variance is the difference between the *standard and actual purchase price for the actual quantity* of materials purchased or used in production.

It is calculated by applying the following formula:

Actual quantity × (Standard price – Actual price)

This may be expanded to:

(Actual quantity × Standard price) – (Actual quantity × Actual price)

Example 19.1

To produce one unit a standard usage of 10 litres of material has been set with a standard price of £3.00 per litre. In the period, 50 units were made and 500 litres of material consumed at a cost of £2.50 per litre.

In this example there is no usage variance because the quantity of material which should have been used for 50 units is 500 litres (50 units × 10 litres) which is the same as the actual usage. We need calculate only the price variance and to demonstrate its application we will use both formulae, starting with the expanded version:

	£
Actual quantity× Standard price	
500 litres× £3.00 per litre	1,500
Actual quantity× Actual price	
500 litres× £2.50 per litre	1,250
Favourable price variance	250

Note that the price variance is favourable because *less* has been spent per unit of materials than was expected.

Using the shorter formula:

Actual quantity × (Standard price – actual price)
= 500 litres × (£3.00 per litre – £2.50 per litre)
= 500 litres × £0.50
= £250 favourable price variance

19.6.2 Direct material usage variance

This variance is the difference between the *standard quantity specified for the actual production* and the *actual quantity used*, at standard purchase price. It is calculated by applying the following formula:

(Standard quantity specified for actual production – Actual quantity used) × Standard price per unit

This may be expanded to:

(Standard quantity for actual production × Standard price) – (Actual quantity × Standard price)

Example 19.2

To produce one unit a standard usage of 10 litres of material has been set with a standard price of £3.00 per litre. In the period, 50 units were made and 600 litres of material consumed at a cost of £3.00 per litre.

In this example there is no price variance because the actual price of material per litre is the same as the standard which has been set. We need calculate only the usage variance and to demonstrate its application we will use both formulae, starting with the expanded version.

	£
Standard quantity × Standard price	
500 litres × £3.00 per litre	1,500
Actual quantity × Standard price	
600 litres × £3.00 per litre	1,800
Adverse material usage variance	(300)

Note that the standard quantity specified for the actual level of production must be calculated by multiplying the standard usage for one unit by the actual number of units produced. The variance is *adverse* because *more* material was used than planned at this level of production.

Using the shorter formula:

(Standard quantity specified for actual production – Actual quantity used) × Standard price per unit

= (500 litres – 600 litres) × £3.00 per litre
= 100 litres × £3.00 per litre
= (£300) adverse material usage variance

In a complex process it may be appropriate further to subdivide the direct material usage variance into the *direct materials mix variance*, which is used when different materials are applied in standard proportions; and the *direct material yield variance*, which is used when output is different from planned, such as in a chemical plant. The formulae are:

Direct material mix variance:
(Quantity in standard mix proportions – Quantity in actual mix) × Standard price.

Direct material yield variance:
(Standard yield of actual input – Actual yield of input) × Standard material cost.

19.6.3 Direct material total variance

This variance is the difference between the *standard direct material cost of the actual production volume* and the *actual cost of direct materials*. It is calculated by applying the following formula:

(Standard units x Standard price) – (Actual units x Actual price)

Example 19.3

To produce one unit a standard usage of 10 litres of material has been set with a standard price of £3.00 per litre. In the period, 70 units were made and 770 litres of material consumed at a cost of £2.80 per litre.

Applying the formula:

	£
Standard units × Standard price	
700 litres × £3.00	2,100
Actual units × Actual price	
770 litres × £2.80	2,156
Adverse direct material total variance	(56)

Note that the standard units in the formula are calculated by multiplying the *actual volume* of production achieved by the *standard per unit* 2 i.e., 70 units × 10 litres. The variance is *adverse* because the actual cost is *higher* than intended for the actual level of production.

The total variance needs to be further subdivided to provide management with useful information and, in this example we can go on to calculate the *price* and *usage variance*.

Material price variance:

Actual quantity × (Standard price – Actual price)
= 770 litres × (£3.00 – £2.80)
= 770 litres × £0.20
= £154 favourable price variance

Material usage variance:

(Standard quantity specified for actual production – Actual quantity used) × Standard price per unit

(700 litres – 770 litres) × £3.00
= 70 litres × £3.00
= (£210) adverse usage variance

The favourable price variance of £154 and the adverse usage variance of (£210) when combined make the *total adverse variance* of (£56).

Without further information, it is difficult to specify the reasons for these variances; we might suggest that the use of an inferior quality material has given a favourable price variance, but this has resulted in a higher level of wastage with an adverse usage variance. If this is the case, the policy of using inferior material, although giving a favourable price variance, has led to the overall position being worse than planned.

19.7 Direct Labour Variances

If material variances are understood, there will be no difficulty in understanding labour variances. Instead of looking at usage and price we are now concerned with the *rates paid to labour* and their *efficiency*. The basic formula is:

Total labour cost = Hours worked × Rate per hour

Standards are set both for the rate per hour and the time required to complete a certain measure of work. The latter is usually measured in *standard hours* or *minutes* and is the quantity of work at standard performance, expressed as a standard unit of work in a standard period of time. For example, it may be decided that a worker can make 100 units in an hour. If in a working day the output is 900 units it can be said that the output is 9 standard hours, irrespective of the actual time taken.

When the production for a period has been completed and the actual total labour cost is compared to the standard labour cost, there is likely to be a difference. This total cost variance may be either because the efficiency of labour used is different from the standard, or because the actual rate paid per hour is different from the standard, or a combination of these two factors.

The total variance can be broken down into a rate variance and an efficiency variance (Figure 19.2).

Fig 19.2   *Labour rate variance and efficiency variance*

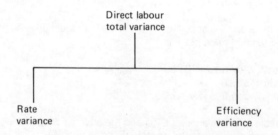

19.8 **Calculation of Direct Labour Variances**

19.8.1 Direct labour rate variance
This variance is the difference between the *standard and actual direct labour rate per hour for the actual hours worked*. It is calculated by applying the following formula:

(Standard rate per hour – Actual rate per hour) × Actual hours

This may be expanded to:

(Standard rate × Actual hours) – (Actual rate × Actual hours)

Example 19.4

The standard for making one unit is 5 standard hours at a standard rate of £4.00 per hour. During the period, 60 units were made which took 300 actual hours at the rate of £3.80 per hour.

Using the short formula:

(Standard rate per hour – Actual rate per hour) × Actual hours

= (£4.00 – £3.80) 300 hours
= £0.20 × 300 hours
= £60 favourable rate variance

This is a *favourable* variance because the actual wage rate was *less* than planned.

19.8.2 Direct labour efficiency variance
This variance is the difference between the *actual production achieved measured in standard hours* and the *actual hours worked*, valued at the standard labour rate. It is calculated by applying the following formula:

(Standard hours produced – Actual hours worked) × Standard rate per hour

This can be expanded to:

(Standard hours produced × Standard rate per hour) – (Actual hours worked × Standard rate per hour)

Example 19.5

The standard for making one unit is 5 standard hours at a standard rate of £4.00 per hour. During the period, 80 units were made which took 360 actual hours at the rate of £4.00 per hour.

Using the short formula:

(Standard hours produced – Actual hours worked) × Standard rate per hour

= (400 – 360) × £4.00 per hour
= 40 × £4.00
= £160 favourable efficiency variance

This is a *favourable* variance because a *greater* output in standard hours was achieved in the hours actually worked.

19.8.3 Direct labour total variance

This variance is standard direct labour cost *minus* the actual direct labour cost incurred for the production achieved. It is calculated by using the following formula:

(Standard direct labour hours produced × Standard rate per hour) – (Actual direct labour hours × Actual rate per hour)

Example 19.6

To make one unit the standard hours are 5 and the standard rate is £4.00 per hour. The actual production is 100 units and this took 480 actual hours at a rate of £4.50 per hour.

Using the formula:

(Standard direct labour hours produced × Standard rate per hour) – (Actual direct labour hours × Actual rate per hour)

= (500 standard hours × £4.00) – (480 hours × £4.50)
= £2,000 – £2,160
= (£160) adverse direct labour total variance

This total variance can be subdivided into a *rate* and an *efficiency* variance.

Direct labour rate variance:

(Standard rate – Actual rate) × Actual hours

= (£4.00 – £4.50) × 450 hours
= (240) adverse rate variance

Direct labour efficiency variance:

(Standard hours – Actual hours) × Standard rate per hour

= (500 – 480) × £4.00
= £80 favourable efficiency variance

Note that the rate and efficiency variances combined agree with the *total variance*.

Exercises

1. What are the advantages of standard costing?
2. Explain the term variance analysis, and its use.
3. The workforce of a company takes 460 actual hours to achieve 500 standard hours of production. The standard wage rate is £4.50 per hour and the actual rate paid is £5.00 per hour. Calculate the relevant variances.
4. For a specified level of production, the standard usage of materials is 25 metres and the standard price is £3.00 per metre. The actual usage is 23 metres and the actual price £3.50 per metre. Calculate the relevant variances.
5. A company produces a product which has a standard variable production cost of £8 per unit made up as follows:

	£/unit
Direct materials	4.60 (2 kilos × £2.30/kilo)
Direct labour	2.10 (0.7 hours × £3.00/hour)
Variable overhead	1.30

Fixed manufacturing costs are treated as period costs. The following information is available for the period just ended:

Variable manufacturing cost of sales (at standard cost)	£263,520
Opening stock of finished goods (at standard cost)	£120,800
Closing stock of finished goods (at standard cost)	£146,080
Direct material price variance	£2,571 unfavourable
Raw materials used in manufacture (at actual cost)	£170,310
Direct labour rate variance	£4,760 unfavourable
Direct labour efficiency variance	£3,240 favourable

Required:
(a) Determine for the period just ended:
  (i) the number of units produced,
  (ii) the raw material usage variance,
  (iii) the total actual direct labour cost, and
  (iv) the actual cost per kilo of raw material used.
(b) Outline the possible causes of the raw material variances.

(ACCA, December 1986)

6. (a) Discuss the factors which should be considered when setting the standard labour cost of a product.

(b) Settah Ltd manufactures two different types of component in two production departments, a press shop and a fitting department.

The budgeted production and standard labour costs for Period 5 were:

	Press Shop	Fitting Dept
Budgeted production:		
Component A	6,000 units	5,000 units
Component B	8,000 units	9,000 units
Standard labour cost per unit:		
Component A	£3	£8
Component B	£6	£6
Standard wage rate per hour	£3	£4
Actual results for Period 5 were:		
Production:		
Component A	4,000 units	6,000 units
Component B	7,800 units	8,600 units
Gross wages paid to direct workers	£60,000	£90,000

Throughout Period 5 there were 135 direct workers employed in the Press Shop and 145 in the Fitting Department. All employees in both departments attended and were paid for a 40 hour week in each of the four weeks in Period 5. However during the final week in the Fitting Department each employee was idle for 3 hours; the result of poor material scheduling.

Required:

Calculate the appropriate direct wage variances for Period 5.

(ACCA, December 1980)

20 Standard Costing – Overhead and Sales Variances

20.1 Introduction

When examining absorption costing in Chapter 7, we saw that overheads could be charged to production in a variety of ways. The budgeted overhead for the period was divided by the appropriate units of base, a measure of time being the preferred method. One method of measuring output is in the form of *standard hours of production*. This is the method we will use when considering overhead variance analysis.

It is possible to calculate variances for the total overheads – that is, fixed and variable overheads combined. Although this is slightly simpler, it is assumed in this chapter that the standard costing system uses total absorption costing principles and that both fixed and variable overheads are absorbed into production costs. It is therefore more sensible to calculate fixed and variable overhead variances separately.

When the standard costing system is based on marginal costing principles, only variable overheads are charged to production. It is therefore necessary to calculate only the variances for the variable overheads.

Sales variances are income variances and if the actual performance is greater than the standard, the difference is a *favourable* variance. The variances are derived from the sales margin because this assists management in their objective of controlling profit.

20.2 Fixed Overhead Variances

The most important point to remember in calculating fixed overhead variances is that fixed overheads *do not change with changes in the level of production*. Overheads are charged to production on the basis of the fixed overhead absorption rate (FOAR) which must be calculated before production starts. The FOAR is therefore calculated from budgeted figures.

The relationship of these variances is shown in Figure 20.1.

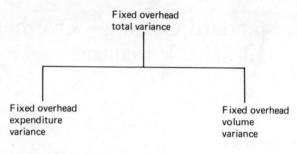

Fig 20.1   *Relationship of fixed overhead variances*

To demonstrate the calculation of these three variances we will use the following data:

Budgeted fixed overheads for the period	£3,000
Budgeted standard hours of production	1,000 hours
Actual fixed overheads for the period	£3,200
Actual standard hours produced	1,100 hours

The first step before calculating any of the variances is to work out the *predetermined overhead absorption rate*:

$$\text{Fixed overhead absorption rate} = \frac{\text{Budgeted fixed overheads}}{\text{Budgeted standard hours}}$$

$$= \frac{£3,000}{1,000 \text{ hours}}$$

$$= £3.00 \text{ per hour}$$

20.2.1 Fixed overhead total variance

This variance is the difference between the *standard cost of fixed overhead charged to production* and the *actual fixed overhead* for the period. It is calculated by using the following formula:

(Standard hours production × FOAR) – Actual fixed overheads

= (1,100 × £3.00) – £3,200
= £100 favourable fixed overhead total variance

Note that the variance is *favourable* because *more* overhead is charged to production than has been incurred.

20.2.2 Fixed overhead expenditure variance
This variance is simply the difference between the *budgeted fixed overhead* and the *actual overhead incurred*. Using the above data:

Budgeted fixed overhead – Actual fixed overhead

= £3,000 – £3,200
= (£200) adverse expenditure variance

20.2.3 Fixed overhead volume variance
This variance is the difference between the *overhead absorbed* in the production achieved and the *budgeted fixed overhead* for the period. It is calculated using the formula:

(Standard hours production × FOAR)– Budgeted fixed overhead

= (1,100 × £3.00) – £3,000
= £300 favourable volume variance

This variance is *favourable* because the actual volume of production was *higher* than the planned volume by 100 standard hours, thus a further £300 was absorbed into production than originally planned.

Note that the combined volume and expenditure variances agree with the *total variance*.

20.3 Variable Overhead Variances

The most important point to remember in calculating variable overhead variances is that the variable overheads should *fluctuate in relation to levels of production*. This means that once the predetermined variable overhead absorption rate (VOAR) has been calculated, the original budgeted figures will lose their relevance (see Figure 20.2 overleaf).

To demonstrate the calculation of these three variances we will use the following data:

Budgeted variable overheads for the period	£2,000
Budgeted standard hours of production	1,000 hours
Actual variable overheads for the period	£2,200
Actual standard hours produced	900 hours
Actual hours worked	850 hours

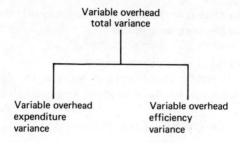

Fig 20.2 *Relationship of variance overhead variances*

The first step before calculating any of the variances is to work out the *predetermined overhead absorption rate*:

$$\text{Variable overhead absorption rate} = \frac{\text{Budgeted variable overheads}}{\text{Budgeted standard hours}}$$

$$= \frac{£2,000}{1,000 \text{ hours}}$$

$$= £2.00 \text{ per hour}$$

For the purpose of calculating the variances, we will not refer to the original budget figures again, but we will use the VOAR.

20.3.1 Variable overhead total variance

This variance is the difference between the *actual variable overheads incurred* and the *actual variable overheads absorbed* for the period. The formula is:

(Standard hours production × VOAR) – Actual variable overheads

= (900 × £2.00) – £2,200
= £1,800 – £2,200
= (£400) adverse total variance

Note that the total variance is *adverse* because only £1,800 is charged to production, but the *actual variable overheads incurred* were £2,200.

20.3.2 Variable overhead expenditure variance

This variance is the difference between the *variable overheads allowed for the actual hours worked* and the *actual overhead incurred*. The formula is:

(Actual hours worked × VOAR) – Actual variable overheads

= (850 × £2.00) – £2,200
= £1,700 – £2,200
= (£500) adverse expenditure variance

Note that the variance is *adverse* because we should have incurred variable overheads of £1,700 on the basis of the actual hours of work, but the *actual overheads* were £2,200.

20.3.3 Variable overhead efficiency variance

This variance is the difference between the *variable overheads allowed for the actual hours worked* and the *variable overhead absorbed in production*. The formula is:

(Actual hours worked × VOAR) – (Standard hours production × VOAR)

= (850 × £2.00) – (900 × £2.00)
= £1,700 – £1,800
= £100 favourable overhead efficiency variance

Note that this is a true efficiency variance: it is *favourable* because *less hours* were actually taken to produce a greater output as measured in standard hours.

The expenditure and efficiency variances combined agree with the *total variance*.

20.4 Fixed and Variable Overhead Variances Compared

It is essential to note that fixed overheads *do not* vary with production levels, but variable overheads *do*.

When calculating overhead variances the comparison for fixed overheads must be with the *original budget*; with variable overheads there is normally a different level of production than the variable overheads *should have been* for the actual hours worked. This can be referred

Fig 20.3 *Comparison of overhead calculations*

VARIANCE	FIXED OVERHEAD	VARIABLE OVERHEAD
Total	Actual overheads — Overheads absorbed	Actual overheads — Overheads absorbed
Expenditure	Actual overheads — Budget overheads	Actual overheads — Allowed overheads
Volume and efficiency	Budget overheads — overheads absorbed	Allowed overheads— Overheads abscribed

to as the 'allowed variable overhead', and Figure 20.3 illustrates the differences.

The other key point is that the overhead absorption rates, both FOAR and VOAR, must be calculated on the *original budgeted figures*. The absorption rate is a predetermined rate, and the actual figures will not be available at the time of calculation.

20.5 **Sales Margin Variances**

Management is interested not only in controlling costs, but also in controlling *income*. The income from sales is controlled by concentrating on the *profit* or *margin from sales*. The variances which can be calculated are shown in Figure 20.4.

The *standard sales margin* is the difference between the standard selling price and the standard costs of production, including both fixed and variable costs. The *actual margin* is the difference between the actual selling price and the *standard costs* of production (NOT the actual costs of production). The three variances are calculated using the data on the next page:

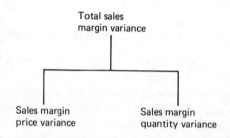

Fig 20.4 *Sales margin price variance and sales margin quantity variance*

	Volume	Selling price per unit	Margin per unit
Budget	400	£10.00	£2.00
Actual	380	£11.00	£3.00

20.5.1 Total sales margin variance

This is the difference between the *budgeted margin* and the *actual margin*, the cost of sales being at the standard cost of production. The formula is:

(Actual sales in units × Actual margin per unit of sales) – (Standard sales in units × standard margin per unit)

Using the above data the calculation is:

(380 × £3.00) – (400 × £2.00)
= £1,140 – £800
= £340 favourable total sales variance

20.5.2 Sales margin price variance

This is the difference between the *actual margin per unit* and the *standard margin per unit* multiplied by the actual sales volume. Both the actual and the standard margins are calculated on the basis of standard unit costs. The formula is:

(Actual margin – Standard margin) × Actual sales volume in units

Applying the formula to the data:

(3.00 – £2.00) × 380
= £380 favourable sales margin price variance

20.5.3 Sales margin volume variance

This is the difference between the *actual sales volume* and the *standard or budgeted sales volume*, both measured in units, multiplied by the standard margin per unit of sales. The formula is:

(Actual sales in units – Standard sales in units) × Standard margin per unit of sales

$= (380 - 400) \times £2.00$

$= (£40)$ adverse sales margin volume variance

Note that the price and volume variance combined agree with the *total variance*. A favourable price variance may well be associated with an adverse volume variance, as the *increase in price* (and thus margin) may *reduce demand*.

Exercises

1. What are the three variable overhead variances, and how are they calculated?

2. A company has the following budget for a financial period:

Variable overheads	£2,000
Standard hours of production	2,000

The actual variable overheads for the period are £1,520 and 1,400 actual hours are worked to produce 1,600 standard hours of production. Calculate the relevant variances.

3. Describe how the three sales margin variances are calculated.

4. Chemico Ltd manufactures and distributes an industrial cleaning compound known as Splodge, the standard direct costs per cylinder of which are:

Material	100 kg of A at 20p per kg
	200 kg of B at 25p per kg
Labour	10 hours at 90p per hour

The budgeted monthly production/sales is 500 cylinders and the selling price is £100 per cylinder.

The following details relate to May 1975 when 510 cylinders of Splodge were produced and sold:

Sales	£50,650
Materials used:	
A 51,600 kg, cost	£10,250
B 101,500 kg, cost	£25,880
Labour:	
5,000 hours, cost	£4,575

You are required to compute

(a) the price and usage variances for each material

(b) the wages rate and efficiency variances

(c) the sales price and volume variances, and to comment briefly upon the information revealed by each of the variances you have computed.

(ACCA, June 1985)

5. *Standard Company*

A company manufactures a number of products, data for one of which are shown below:

Standard cost

Direct materials	8 units @ £2 per unit
Direct labour	4 hours @ £5 per hour
Production overhead	4 hours @ £6 per hour
Administration and selling overhead	50% of production cost
Profit	$16\frac{2}{3}$% of selling price

Budget for April

Sales	5,000 units
Production	5,200 units

Actual results during April

Sales	5,150 units valued at £566,500
Direct materials used	£77,040
Direct labour costs	£110,770
Production overhead incurred	£122,800

Variances calculated in April

Direct materials	price £8,560F
	usage £800A
Direct labour	rate £6,270A
	efficiency £1,500F

You are required to calculate the:

(a) actual output;
(b) actual price per unit of direct material;
(c) actual rate per hour of direct labour;
(d) overhead expenditure variance;
(e) overhead volume variance;
(f) selling price variance
(g) sales volume profit variance.

(*CIMA, May 1986*)

21 Capital Investment Appraisal

21.1 Introduction

When management is considering the investment of a large sum of money over a number of years, the fundamental objective is to ensure that the total monies received over time are *higher* than the amount of the original investment.

In these circumstances, the distinction between fixed and variable costs is probably of small importance. What will be critical is the timing and amounts of *cash flows* and, above all, the *degree of risk*.

To evaluate these long-term projects there are a number of techniques which are considered in this chapter, together with their advantages and disadvantages.

21.2 Payback Technique

With this technique, it is necessary to find out the *time it takes for the cash flowing in to equal that flowing out*. Normally the project with the shortest **payback period** – that is, the one which pays back the investment *fastest* – is chosen.

To calculate the payback period the cash inflows and outflows are identified both in amount and timing. The *net cash flow* (**NCF**) is then calculated.

Example 21.1

A company has a choice of three projects, each requiring an investment of £20,000 to be paid at the beginning of the project, although one project has a different time span. The net cash flows and lengths of the projects are:

Year	Project A £	Project B £	Project C £
1	10,000	7,000	10,000
2	8,000	7,000	4,000
3	2,000	6,000	4,000
4	1,000	2,000	4,000
5	–	–	8,000

Payback periods:

	Years
Project A	3
Project B	3
Project C	3.5

Projects A and B are ranked equal, although there is a significant difference in the timing of the net cash flows over the period. Project C is ranked last as it takes 3.5 years to repay the investment. The fact that Project C shows a greater total return of cash is not taken into account.

20.2.1 Disadvantages of the technique

1. No recognition is made of the amounts of cash which may be received *after* the payback period.
2. The actual *incidence* of the net cash flows is ignored. For example, does the net cash flow of £6,000 in year 3 for Project B have any significance which should be accounted for?

21.2.2 Advantages of the technique

1. The future is uncertain and the sooner the investment is recovered the *smaller the risk* involved.
2. It is simple to understand and apply; this may be why it is the *most used technique* in industry.
3. The quickest paying project is selected, which can be an advantage in times of *cash shortages*.
4. Cash is more important than accounting profits in investment appraisal and the benefits of the technique is that it uses *cash flows*.
5. If there is rapid technological change, projects with the most *rapid turn round* are favoured.

21.3 Accounting Rate of Return (ARR)

This technique departs from the emphasis on cash, as ARR is calculated by expressing the *average profits*, after depreciation, as a *percentage of the capital invested*. There are variations on this definition, but the basic principles are the same. The same projects are used as in Example 21.1. We will assume that the investment of £20,000 is charged in full as depreciation to arrive at the profit figures.

Year	Project A £	Project B £	Project C £
1	10,000	7,000	10,000
2	8,000	7,000	4,000
3	2,000	6,000	4,000
4	1,000	2,000	4,000
5	–	–	8,000
Total net cash flow	21,000	22,000	30,000
Less depreciation	20,000	20,000	20,000
Profit	1,000	2,000	10,000
Average profits	250	500	2,000
ARR based on £20,000 investment	1.25%	2.5%	10%

On the criteria employed in this technique, Project C would be chosen as it has the highest ARR.

21.3.1 Advantages of the technique

1. The calculations are *simple*.
2. The *entire life of the project* is taken into account.

21.3.2 Disadvantages of the technique

1. The *timing of cash movements* is completely ignored.
2. There are a number of different definitions of the term 'Accounting Rate of Return', and various ways of calculating it, which can lead to *confusion*.
3. The crucial factor in investment decisions is cash flow, and ARR uses *profit*.

21.4 Discounted Cash Flow

The most sophisticated of the techniques for investment appraisal is discounted cash flow (**DCF**). This uses the concept that £1.00 in a year's time will not have the same value as £1.00 *now*. Ignoring the impact of inflation, the principle is that £1.00 that is available now can be invested immediately and by the end of the year its value will have grown by the amount of the interest gained. Because of this interest, paying £1.00 now in anticipation of receiving £1.00 in one year's time is unprofitable. With an interest rate of 100% only 50p would need to be invested in return for £1.00 in one year's time and only 25p for £1.00 in two years' time.

The principle that £1.00 in a year's time is not worth £1.00 now can be likened to using different currencies; a *conversion rate* is needed to ensure that all the £1.00s have the same value. This is done by converting future cash flows from the project into equivalent values as at the present time, usually by using discount tables. The two primary methods are *Net Present Value* (**NPV**) and *Internal Rate of Return* (**IRR**).

21.4.1 Net present value

This method converts the future net cash flows into present day values. The project with the *largest net present value* is the one preferred, as Example 21.2 shows.

Example 21.2

A company has a choice of one of two projects, both involving an investment of £20,000 with net cash flows as shown below. The current cost of capital is 10%.

Year		Project A £	Project B £
1		1,000	14,000
2		2,000	4,000
3		2,000	4,000
4		7,000	2,000
5		20,000	8,000

Year	Discount factor 10%	Project A		Project B	
		Net cash flow £	Present value £	Net cash flow £	Present value £
0	1.000	(20,000)	(20,000)	(20,000)	(20,000)
1	0.909	1,000	909	14,000	12,726
2	0.826	2,000	1,652	4,000	3,304
3	0.751	2,000	1,502	4,000	3,004
4	0.683	7,000	4,781	2,000	1,366
5	0.621	20,000	12,420	8,000	4,968
Net present value			1,264		5,368

Select Project B, as it gives the highest net present value.

The following points should be noted:

1. The NPV calculation layout is suitable for most problems, and should be *memorised*.
2. All cash flows are taken to occur at the *end of the year* except for the initial investment. This is normally so large that an error would result if it were treated at the end of year 1 and the discount rate applied. To overcome this problem the convention is to show the initial invest- ment in year 0.
3. The £5,368 from Project B is the present value of the ultimate benefit arising from the project if money is borrowed at 10%.
4. The discount factor is obtained from a set of tables (Appendix A). The rate of 10% was selected because we are told that the cost of capital was that amount. Other criteria may be used by a company to determine the discount factor.

21.4.2 Internal rate of return

The internal rate of return, also known as discounted yield, uses the same principles, but the aim of the method is to find the discount rate which gives a *net present value of 0* for a project.

The two projects in Example 21.2 both gave a *positive net present value* using a discount rate of 10%. This means that their internal rate of return must be higher than 10%. As the exact rate is not known, the figures must be recalculated using a higher discount rate to see whether that gives a zero net present value.

The correct discount rate is unlikely to be selected by chance. We will start by taking a rate that we think will be in excess of the internal rate of return, which should therefore give a negative net present value.

Year	Discount factor 20%	Project A		Project B	
		Net cash flow £	Present value £	Net cash flow £	Present value £
0	1.000	(20,000)	(20,000)	(20,000)	(20,000)
1	0.833	1,000	833	14,000	11,662
2	0.694	2,000	1,388	4,000	2,776
3	0.579	2,000	1,158	4,000	2,316
4	0.482	7,000	3,374	2,000	964
5	0.402	20,000	8,040	8,000	3,216
Net present value			(5,207)		934

Project B still has a positive net present value so the internal rate of return must be above 20%; with Project A the internal rate of return must fall somewhere between 10 and 20%. The calculation is:

	£
Net Present Value at 10%	1,264
Net Present Value at 20%	(5,207)
Range of the present values	6,471

Difference between the two discount rates = 10%.

$$\text{IRR} = \frac{£1,264}{£6,471} \times 10\% = 1.95\%$$

Therefore the IRR is 1.95% along the range of present values. As the lowest discount factor used was 10%, the IRR is 10% + 1.95% which equals approximately 12%.

21.4.3 Comparison of NPV and IRR

The internal rate of return, being relative, is a measure of the *intensity of capital use*; if capital is limited, it is better to invest in high rate projects. The IRR also gives a return for *risk*. With Project A, if the cost of capital is 10% and the IRR is 12%, the return for risk is 2%.

202 *Cost and Management Accounting*

The IRR is a slightly more difficult method to apply than net present value. In most cases, both methods will give the same answer as to acceptance or rejection, but may vary on ranking, thus leading to different selections.

Care should be taken in basing a decision on the internal rate of return. Although an IRR of 30% may appear enticing, if the return is on an investment of only £5.00 then an IRR of 20% on an investment of £5,000 is more sensible. The selection of a project with the highest IRR, particularly if of a short life, implies that at the end of the project other investment opportunities will present themselves with the same, or higher, returns.

Exercises

1. What financial decisions will management take into account when making capital investment decisions?
2. What are the advantages and disadvantages of the payback technique?
3. Explain the principles underlying the discounted cash flow technique.
4. A company has the choice of one of two projects, each with a life span of 4 years and requiring an initial investment of £6,000. Select the best project by using the net present value technique at a discount rate of 10%. The net cash flows for the two projects are:

Year	Project A £	Project B £
1	2,000	4,000
2	3,000	3,000
3	3,000	3,000
4	4,000	1,000

Appendix A: Present Value Tables

Present value of 1 at compound interest: $(1 + r)^{-n}$

Years (n)	Interest rates (r) 1	2	3	4	5	6	7	8	9	10	11	12	13	14	15
1	0.9901	0.9804	0.9709	0.9615	0.9524	0.9434	0.9346	0.9259	0.9174	0.0901	0.9009	0.8929	0.8850	0.8772	0.8696
2	0.9803	0.9612	0.9426	0.9246	0.9070	0.8900	0.8734	0.8573	0.8417	0.8264	0.8116	0.7972	0.7831	0.7695	0.7561
3	0.9706	0.9423	0.9151	0.8890	0.8638	0.8396	0.8163	0.7938	0.7722	0.7513	0.7312	0.7118	0.6931	0.6750	0.6575
4	0.9610	0.9238	0.8885	0.8548	0.8227	0.7921	0.7629	0.7350	0.7084	0.6830	0.6587	0.6355	0.6133	0.5921	0.5718
5	0.9515	0.9057	0.8626	0.8219	0.7835	0.7473	0.7130	0.6806	0.6499	0.6209	0.5935	0.5674	0.5428	0.5194	0.4972
6	0.9420	0.8880	0.8375	0.7903	0.7462	0.7050	0.6663	0.6302	0.5963	0.5645	0.5346	0.5066	0.4803	0.4556	0.4323
7	0.9327	0.8706	0.8131	0.7599	0.7107	0.6651	0.6227	0.5835	0.5470	0.5132	0.4817	0.4523	0.4251	0.3996	0.3759
8	0.9235	0.8535	0.7894	0.7307	0.6768	0.6274	0.5820	0.5403	0.5019	0.4665	0.4339	0.4039	0.3762	0.3506	0.3269
9	0.9143	0.8368	0.7684	0.7026	0.6446	0.5919	0.5439	0.5002	0.4604	0.4241	0.3909	0.3606	0.3329	0.3075	0.2834
10	0.9053	0.8203	0.7441	0.6756	0.6139	0.5584	0.5083	0.4632	0.4224	0.3855	0.3522	0.3220	0.2946	0.2697	0.2472
11	0.8963	0.8043	0.7224	0.6496	0.5847	0.5268	0.4751	0.4289	0.3875	0.3505	0.3173	0.2875	0.2607	0.2366	0.2149
12	0.8874	0.7885	0.7014	0.6246	0.5568	0.4970	0.4440	0.3971	0.3555	0.3188	0.2858	0.2567	0.2307	0.2076	0.1869
13	0.8787	0.7730	0.6810	0.6006	0.5303	0.4688	0.4150	0.3677	0.3262	0.2862	0.2575	0.2292	0.2042	0.1821	0.1625
14	0.8700	0.7579	0.6611	0.5775	0.5051	0.4423	0.3878	0.3405	0.2992	0.2633	0.2320	0.2046	0.1807	0.5197	0.1413
15	0.8613	0.7430	0.6419	0.5553	0.4810	0.4173	0.3624	0.3152	0.2745	0.2394	0.2090	0.1827	0.1599	0.1401	0.1229
16	0.8528	0.7284	0.6232	0.5339	0.4581	0.3936	0.3387	0.2919	0.2519	0.2176	0.1883	0.1631	0.1415	0.1229	0.1069
17	0.8444	0.7142	0.6050	0.5134	0.4363	0.3714	0.3168	0.2703	0.2311	0.1978	0.1696	0.1456	0.1252	0.1078	0.0929
18	0.8360	0.7002	0.5874	0.4936	0.4155	0.3503	0.2959	0.2502	0.2120	0.1799	0.1528	0.1300	0.1108	0.0946	0.0808
19	0.8277	0.6864	0.5703	0.4746	0.3957	0.3305	0.2765	0.2317	0.1945	0.1635	0.1377	0.1161	0.0980	0.0829	0.0703
20	0.8195	0.6730	0.5537	0.4564	0.3769	0.3118	0.2584	0.2145	0.1784	0.1486	0.1240	0.1037	0.0868	0.0728	0.0611
25	0.7795	0.6095	0.4776	0.3751	0.2953	0.2330	0.1842	0.1460	0.1160	0.0923	0.0736	0.0588	0.0471	0.0378	0.0304
30	0.7419	0.5521	0.4120	0.3083	0.2314	0.1741	0.1314	0.0994	0.0754	0.0573	0.0437	0.0334	0.0256	0.0196	0.0151
35	0.7059	0.5000	0.3554	0.2534	0.1813	0.1301	0.0937	0.0676	0.0490	0.0356	0.0259	0.0189	0.0139	0.0102	0.0075
40	0.6717	0.4529	0.3066	0.2083	0.1420	0.0972	0.0668	0.0460	0.0318	0.0221	0.0154	0.0107	0.0075	0.0053	0.0037
45	0.6391	0.4102	0.2644	0.1712	0.1113	0.0727	0.0476	0.0313	0.0207	0.0137	0.0091	0.0061	0.0041	0.0027	0.0019
50	0.6080	0.3715	0.2281	0.1407	0.0872	0.0543	0.0339	0.0213	0.0134	0.0085	0.0054	0.0035	0.0022	0.0014	0.0009

	16	17	18	19	20	21	22	23	24	25	26	27	28	29	30
1	0.8621	0.8547	0.8475	0.8403	0.8333	0.8264	0.8197	0.8130	0.8065	0.8000	0.7937	0.7874	0.7812	0.7752	0.7692
2	0.7432	0.7305	0.7182	0.7062	0.6944	0.6830	0.6719	0.6610	0.6504	0.6400	0.6299	0.6200	0.6104	0.6009	0.5917
3	0.6407	0.6244	0.6086	0.5934	0.5787	0.5645	0.5507	0.5374	0.5245	0.5120	0.4999	0.4882	0.4768	0.4658	0.4552
4	0.5523	0.5337	0.5158	0.4987	0.4823	0.4665	0.4514	0.4369	0.4230	0.4069	0.3968	0.3844	0.3725	0.3611	0.3501
5	0.4761	0.4561	0.4371	0.4190	0.4019	0.3855	0.3700	0.3552	0.3411	0.3277	0.3149	0.3027	0.2910	0.2799	0.2693
6	0.4104	0.3898	0.3704	0.3521	0.3349	0.3186	0.3033	0.2888	0.2751	0.2621	0.2499	0.2338	0.2274	0.2170	0.2072
7	0.3538	0.3332	0.3139	0.2959	0.2791	0.2633	0.2486	0.2348	0.2218	0.2097	0.1983	0.1877	0.1776	0.1682	0.1594
8	0.3050	0.2848	0.2660	0.2487	0.2326	0.2176	0.2038	0.1909	0.1789	0.1678	0.1574	0.1478	0.1388	0.1304	0.1226
9	0.2630	0.2434	0.2255	0.2090	0.1938	0.1799	0.1670	0.1552	0.1443	0.1342	0.1249	0.1164	0.1084	0.1011	0.0943
10	0.2267	0.2080	0.1911	0.1756	0.1615	0.1486	0.1369	0.1262	0.1164	0.1074	0.0992	0.0916	0.0847	0.0784	0.0725
11	0.1954	0.1778	0.1619	0.1476	0.1346	0.1228	0.1122	0.1026	0.0938	0.0859	0.0787	0.0721	0.0662	0.0607	0.0558
12	0.1685	0.1520	0.1372	0.1240	0.1122	0.1015	0.0920	0.0834	0.0757	0.0687	0.0625	0.0568	0.0517	0.0471	0.0429
13	0.1452	0.1299	0.1163	0.1042	0.0935	0.0839	0.0754	0.0678	0.0610	0.0550	0.0496	0.0447	0.0404	0.0365	0.0330
14	0.1252	0.1110	0.0985	0.0876	0.0779	0.0693	0.0618	0.0551	0.0492	0.0440	0.0393	0.0352	0.0316	0.0283	0.0254
15	0.1079	0.0949	0.0835	0.0736	0.0649	0.0573	0.0507	0.0448	0.0397	0.0352	0.0312	0.0277	0.0247	0.0219	0.0195
16	0.0930	0.0811	0.0708	0.0618	0.0541	0.0474	0.0415	0.0364	0.0320	0.0281	0.0248	0.0218	0.0193	0.0170	0.0150
17	0.0802	0.0693	0.0600	0.0520	0.0451	0.0391	0.0340	0.0296	0.0258	0.0225	0.0197	0.0172	0.0150	0.0132	0.0116
18	0.0691	0.0592	0.0508	0.0437	0.0376	0.0323	0.0279	0.0241	0.0208	0.0180	0.0156	0.0135	0.0118	0.0102	0.0089
19	0.0596	0.0506	0.0431	0.0367	0.0313	0.0267	0.0229	0.0196	0.0168	0.0144	0.0124	0.0107	0.0092	0.0079	0.0068
20	0.0514	0.0433	0.0365	0.0308	0.0261	0.0221	0.0187	0.0159	0.0135	0.0115	0.0098	0.0084	0.0072	0.0061	0.0053
25	0.0245	0.0197	0.0160	0.0129	0.0105	0.0085	0.0069	0.0057	0.0046	0.0038	0.0031	0.0025	0.0021	0.0017	0.0014
30	0.0116	0.0090	0.0070	0.0054	0.0042	0.0033	0.0026	0.0020	0.0016	0.0012	0.0010	0.0008	0.0006	0.0005	0.0004
35	0.0055	0.0041	0.0030	0.0023	0.0017	0.0013	0.0009	0.0007	0.0005	0.0004	0.0003	0.0002	0.0002	0.0001	0.0001
40	0.0026	0.0019	0.0013	0.0010	0.0007	0.0005	0.0004	0.0003	0.0002	0.0001	0.0001	0.0001	0.0001	0.0000	0.0000
45	0.0013	0.0009	0.0006	0.0004	0.0003	0.0002	0.0001	0.0001	0.0001	0.0000	0.0000	0.0000	0.0000	0.0000	0.0000
50	0.0006	0.0004	0.0003	0.0002	0.0001	0.0001	0.0000	0.0000	0.0000	0.0000	0.0000	0.0000	0.0000	0.0000	0.0000

Appendix B: Glossary

ABSORPTION COSTING – also known as full costing, charges direct costs to the product and allocates or apportions indirect costs to arrive at the full cost of the product.

AVERAGE COST METHOD – prices issues of materials by adding the total of the WIP valuation to the current period costs.

BATCH COSTING – a variation of job costing whereby a number of identical cost units are treated as one batch throughout one or more stages of production.

BREAK-EVEN ANALYSIS – studies the relationship between costs, volumes and profit at different levels of activity.

BUDGETARY CONTROL – the establishment of budgets relating the responsibilities of executives to the requirements of a policy, and the continuous comparison of actual with budgeted results, either to secure by individual action the objectives of that policy, or to provide a basis for its revision.

BY-PRODUCTS – have a relatively small value and arise incidentally in the course of production of the main products.

CONTINUOUS OPERATION COSTING – used where the goods or services being costed are the result of continuous or repetitive operations or processes.

CONTINUOUS STOCKTAKING – where some items of stock are physically counted every day so that all stock is checked at least once in a year.

CONTRACT COSTING – a form of job costing; here work is carried out to the specific requirements of customers and the contract is of long duration.

CONTRIBUTION – the difference between sales and marginal costs.

CONTROLLABLE COSTS – can be regulated by the specific manager with responsibility for that cost.

COST ACCOUNTING – collects and orders data to provide budgets, standards and the actual costs of operations, departments or products.

COST BEHAVIOUR – the way that costs may vary with different levels of activity or volume.

COST CENTRE – a location, function or item of equipment in respect of which costs may be ascertained and related to cost units for control purposes (*ICMA Terminology*).

COST UNIT – a quantitative unit of product or service in relation to which costs are ascertained (*ICMA Terminology*).

COST–VOLUME–PROFIT (C–V–P) ANALYSIS – concerned with the relationship between activity and costs in order to ascertain the most profitable level of activity in the short term.

DIRECT COSTS – can be identified directly with a specific batch, product, service or job.

DIRECT EXPENSES – such items as subcontract work or special tools or equipment bought for a particular job.

DIRECT LABOUR – converts the direct materials into the finished goods, and the time spent on cost units may be calculated from time sheets, job cards or computerised records.

DIRECT MATERIALS – part of the finished goods and can be charged direct to the cost unit.

DISCOUNTED CASH FLOW (DCF) – a capital investment technique which discounts future cash flows to their present-day values.

DISTRIBUTION COSTS – those costs incurred from receipt of the finished goods from the production department to delivery to the customer.

DISTRIBUTION OVERHEADS – those indirect costs arising from the activity of getting the cost unit to the customer.

FINANCIAL ACCOUNTING – concerned with classifying and recording actual transactions in monetary terms to provide a true-and-fair view of an organisation over a period of time or at the end of that time.

FIRST IN, FIRST OUT (FIFO) – a method of pricing issues of materials from stores which uses the price of the first delivery of materials to the company until that particular consignment is exhausted, then uses the price of the next delivery.

FIXED COSTS – in total, stay the same over a wide range of activity for a given period.

FLEXIBLE BUDGET – changes in accordance with levels of activity and reflects the different behaviours of fixed and variable costs.

GOODS RECEIVED NOTE (GRN) – an internal document raised when goods or services are received and compared with the purchase order.

INCREMENTAL COSTS – the additional costs arising from the production or sale of additional units.

INDIRECT COSTS – cannot be identified with any one particular cost unit, but have to be shared over those units to which they are common or by which they are jointly incurred.

INTEGRATED ACCOUNTS – combine the financial and cost accounts through one unified accounting system with only one ledger being maintained.

INTERLOCKING ACCOUNTS – maintain separate ledgers for the financial accounts and cost accounts with each ledger having a control account.

INTERNAL RATE OF RETURN (YIELD) – a method of evaluating capital projects by calculating a percentage.

JOB CARDS – refer to a single job or batch and show the times spent by all employees working on that particular job.

JOB COSTING – used where work is carried out to the specific requirements of customers and the job is of short duration.

JOINT PRODUCT COSTING – used when two or more products are produced from the same process, using the same commonly processed materials up to their point of separation.

JOINT PRODUCTS – two or more products, each with a significant value, which have been produced simultaneously in the course of production.

LAST IN, FIRST OUT (LIFO) – a method of pricing issues of materials from stores which uses the price of the last delivery of materials to the company until that particular consignment is exhausted, then uses the price of the previous delivery.

LIMITING FACTOR – also known as key factor or principal budget factor, is that factor which prevents a company expanding indefinitely or constantly increasing its profits.

MANAGEMENT ACCOUNTING – concerned with providing information to managers so that policies can be formulated, activities planned and controlled, decisions or alternative courses of action taken, assets safeguarded and the activities of the enterprise reported to interested parties.

MARGINAL COST (VARIABLE COST) – is considered in accounting to be the average variable cost and is assumed to be constant in the short term.

MARGINAL COSTING – also known as variable costing or direct costing, is where the variable costs only are charged to cost units and the fixed costs for a financial period are written off in total against the contribution for that period.

MARGIN OF SAFETY – the amount by which sales may decrease before the break-even point is reached and losses begin to arise.

MATERIALS REQUISITION – an internal document authorising the issue from stores of a specified quantity of materials.

MATERIALS RETURN NOTE – an internal document recording the return of unused materials to store.

NEGATIVE CASH FLOW – the cash and cheques being paid out by an organisation.

NET CASH FLOW (NCF) – the difference between the positive and negative cash flows.

NET PRESENT VALUE (NPV) – a method of evaluating capital projects by selecting a discount rate to express future cash flows in present-day monetary terms.

NET REALISABLE VALUE – the actual or estimated selling price of stock net of any trade discounts, from which is deducted any cost incurred to put the stock into a saleable condition, and to which is added all costs incurred in the marketing, selling and distribution of such stock.

OPERATION COSTING – used where goods or services result from a sequence of continuous operations or processes producing normally identical units.

OPPORTUNITY COSTS – the benefits which are sacrificed as a result of selecting one alternative to another.

OVERHEAD ABSORPTION – also known as overhead recovery, is the process by which overheads for a financial period are shared out amongst all the cost units produced in that period.

OVERHEAD ABSORPTION RATE – a method of charging overheads to production.

OVERHEAD ANALYSIS – the charging of overheads to the appropriat cost centres by a process of allocation and apportionment.

OVERHEADS – indirect material, indirect labour and indirect expense costs.

PAYBACK PERIOD – forms the basis of a technique of capital invest-ment appraisal where the project recovering the cash outlay soonest is favoured.

PERIODIC STOCKTAKING – where the physical quantities of ma-terials of all types is counted at a specific date.

PERPETUAL INVENTORY – a system whereby the physical balance of materials is calculated after each issue or receipt. Continuous stock-taking must be in operation to ensure that records reflect actual stock.

PIECEWORK TICKETS – record employees time by each job having a number of piecework tickets attached to it referring to each stage of manufacture.

POSITIVE CASH FLOW – the cash and cheques coming into an organisation.

PROCESS COSTING – a method of costing used where goods or services result from a sequence of continuous or repetitive operations or processes to which costs are charged before being averaged over the units produced during the period (*ICMA Terminology*).

PRODUCTION COSTS – those costs incurred from receipt of the raw materials to completion of the finished product.

PRODUCTION OVERHEADS – those indirect costs arising from the provision of the production resources.

PURCHASE ORDER – sent by the Purchase Department to outside suppliers requesting specific goods or services.

PURCHASE REQUISITION – an official request from production, stores or departments to the Purchase Department detailing require-ments for specific materials, equipment or services.

RELEVANT COSTS – costs appropriate to aiding the making of speci-fic management decisions.

REPLACEMENT PRICE METHOD – uses the replacement price on the day of issue to value materials issued from stores.

RETENTION MONIES – a proportion of the contract value withheld by the client for a certain period after the completion of the contract.

SALES OVERHEADS – those indirect costs arising from the selling of the cost unit.

SELLING COSTS – those costs incurred from receipt of the raw ma-terials to completion of the finished product.

SEMI-VARIABLE COSTS – those costs which do not change in total in direct relationship to changes in the level of activity, neither do they remain fixed.

SERVICE COSTING – used when specific functions or services are costed.

SPECIFIC ORDER COSTING – used where production results are in units, or products which are normally different from each other and consist of easily identifiable contracts or batches.

STANDARD COST – a cost which is a predetermined specified working condition.

STANDARD COSTING – a technique whereby actual costs incurred are compared predetermined standard and the variances analysed.

STANDARD PRICE METHOD – uses a predetermined price to value all issues and receipts of materials from and to stores.

STATEMENTS OF STANDARD ACCOUNTING PRACTICE (SSAPs) – issued by the Accounting Standards Committee and determine the way that certain matters must be treated in financial records and statements.

STOCK RECORD CARD – a record giving not only the physical stock balance, but also outstanding orders and unfulfilled requirements and thus the pre-stock position.

SUNK COSTS – those costs which have been incurred by a past decision and will be unaffected by the present choice between different alternatives.

TIME SHEETS – completed by employees on a weekly or daily basis and countersigned by their supervisor to record time spent on production activities.

VARIABLE COSTS – in total, vary in direct proportion to the volume of activity.

VARIANCE ANALYSIS – the investigation of the differences arising between actual costs incurred and the predetermined standard costs.

Appendix C: Outline Answers to Exercises

3.4 FIFO 100 units at £16 = £1,600
LIFO (50 units at £15) + (50 units at £16) = £1,550

4.3 12 piecework hours at £3 = £36

6.4 Production Department No. 1 £2,317
Production Department No. 2 £2,023

7.4

Job No. 241Z

		£
Materials		300
Wages		175
Overheads		
	A (20 hours @ £4)	80
	B (50 hours @ £5)	250
		805

8.4 Cost of Job £413
Selling price £500
Profit £87 (21%)

9.4 Cost of work £163,000
Profit on contract to date £34,058
Profit in suspense £12,942

11.4 Value of work in progress £8,725
Value of completed units £51,276

12.3

	Product X	Product Y	Total
Profit	£420	£240	£660
Profit/sales	25%	31%	27%

12.4

	Product X	Product Y	Total
Profit	£451	£209	£660
Profit/sales	27%	27%	27%

13.2 Fixed costs £15,000, variable costs £12,000

13.4   *Outline Marginal Cost Statement*

	120,000 units	1 unit
	£	£
Sales	600,000	5
Variable costs	480,000	4
Contribution	120,000	1
Fixed costs	100,000	—
Profit	20,000	

14.3 Variable costs of component   £5.00
Lost contribution   £2.00

Total cost   £7.00

Outside supplier's price is £6.80, so BUY

14.4 (a)   Selling price   £5.00
         Variable costs   £4.40

         Contribution   £0.60

         ACCEPT

    (b) Current total contribution (£5,000 @ £1.60) = £8,000
       Proposed total contribution (7,000 @ £1.10) = £7,700
       REJECT

15.3 $\dfrac{£10,000 + £2,000}{£2}$ = 6,000 units @ £5 = £30,000

    or

$\dfrac{£12,000 \times £5}{£2}$ = £30,000

15.4 Break-even point = 10,000 units
Profit at 15,000 units = £25,000
Margin of safety = 5,000 units

16.4 Absorption costing profit = £2,000
Marginal costing profit = £1,500

18.3

	Jan.	Feb.	Mar.	Apr.	May	Jun.
	£	£	£	£	£	£
Cash in	1,500	15,000	15,000	15,500	20,000	20,000
Cash out	11,500	8,500	13,500	13,500	12,500	15,500

19.3 Labour rate variance £230 Adverse
Labour efficiency variance £180 Favourable
Total labour variance £50 Adverse

19.4 Material price variance £11.50 Adverse
Material usage variance £6.00 Favourable
Total material variance £5.50 Adverse

20.2 Expenditure variance £120 Adverse
Efficiency variance £200 Favourable
Total variance £80 Favourable

21.4 Project A Net present value £3,281
Project B Net present value £3,050

Index

JOHN ALDER
Constitutional and Administrative Law is a clear and readable account of the basic principles of constitutional law. It will be an invaluable introduction to the subject for first-year law-degree students and a self-contained text for 'A'-level and Part One professional examinations, as well as for the interested general reader.

JOHN BINGHAM
Data Processing is a self-contained and up-to-date book, ideal for the relevant business and accounting courses or anyone in business who wishes to improve existing knowledge and skills.

MARISE CREMONA
Criminal Law provides a short but thorough overview of the fundamentals of English criminal law as required for degree courses and professional examinations. It will also prove invaluable reading for magistrates, police officers, social workers and others who need an introduction to the key features of this subject.

E. C. EYRE
Office Administration is suitable for all syllabuses in office administration and relevant parts of business administration and management courses. It is an invaluable text for students studying for the examinations of the Institute of Administrative Management, the Institute of Chartered Secretaries and Administrators, the Society of Company and Commercial Accountants, BTEC and NEBBS.

KATE GREEN
Land Law provides a clear and straightforward introduction to basic English land-law rules. It will be an invaluable text for first-year undergraduates and those studying for professional examinations in both law and other subjects where an understanding of land law is essential.

ROGER OLDCORN
Management is a clear accessible text which will appeal as a self-contained text to students on BTEC, SCOTVEC, Diploma in Management Studies and Institute of Personnel Management courses and as introductory reading for higher-level courses. It will also prove invaluable reading for practising or aspiring managers.

KATE WILLIAMS
Study Skills offers students practical, step-by-step suggestions and strategies to use in their studies, whether these are academic, professional or vocational in nature.

All these books are available at your local bookshop or, in case of difficulty, from John Darvill, Globe Education, Houndmills, Basingstoke, Hampshire RG21 2XS (Tel: 0256 29242).